MW00465665

THE BEST
BEARS EARS
NATIONAL
MONUMENT
HIKES

MORGAN SJOGREN

The Colorado Mountain Club Press
Golden, Colorado

The most notable area landmark is named
"Bears Ears" in every native regional language.

The Best Bears Ears National Monument Hikes
© 2018 by The Colorado Mountain Club

PUBLISHED BY

The Colorado Mountain Club Press
710 Tenth Street, Suite 200, Golden, Colorado 80401
303-996-2743   email: cmcpress@cmc.org
website: http://www.cmc.org

Founded in 1912, The Colorado Mountain Club is the largest outdoor
recreation, education, and conservation organization in the Rocky
Mountains. Look for our books at your local bookstore or outdoor retailer
or online at www.cmcpress.org/.

CORRECTIONS: We greatly appreciate when readers alert us to errors or
outdated information by contacting us at cmcpress@cmc.org.

Morgan Sjogren and Michael Versteeg: photographers
Takeshi Takahashi: designer
Jodi Jennings: copyeditor
Clyde Soles: publisher

 COVER PHOTO: The Citadel, Mike Endres

 DISTRIBUTED TO THE BOOK TRADE BY
Mountaineers Books, 1001 Klickitat Way, Suite 201, Seattle, WA
98134, 800-553-4453, www.mountaineersbooks.org

 We gratefully acknowledge the financial support of the people of
Colorado through the Scientific and Cultural Facilities District
of greater metropolitan Denver for our publishing activities.

TOPOGRAPHIC MAPS are created with CalTopo.com software.

WARNING: Although there has been an effort to make the trail descriptions
in this book as accurate as possible, some discrepancies may exist between the
text and the trails in the field. Hiking in the desert and mountains involves
some risks. This guidebook is not a substitute for your experience and common sense. The users of this guidebook assume full responsibility for their own
safety. Weather, terrain conditions, and individual technical abilities must be
considered before undertaking any of the routes in this guide.

Printed in USA

ISBN: 978-1-937052-53-9

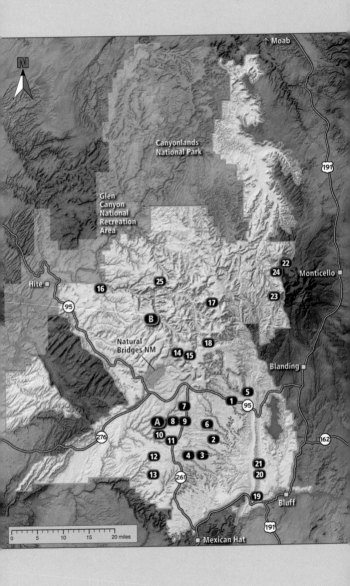

CONTENTS

THE HIKES

Bears Ears is a massive wilderness preserve in a rapidly shrinking natural world.

Foreword

I came to Bears Ears for the first time in 2016, just before President Barack Obama's national monument designation. Something strangely familiar seemed to call me here as I watched the sandstone walls of Indian Creek light ablaze in an orange glow at dusk. Four months later, in February 2017, I returned during a blizzard and attempted to run to the top of the Bears Ears. I didn't get far, and I didn't see much more than a cold blanket of white. Yet Bears Ears triggered something deep inside me that needed to not only return, but to stay. It became my quest to experience, explore, and cover as much ground as possible in this 1.35-million-acre landscape—an impossible task in one lifetime, which made it all the more desirous!

I spent most of 2017 living out of my Jeep and covering hundreds of miles within the original boundaries, encountering more cultural sites and wildlife than humans. The longer I stayed and the deeper I got, the more concerned I became about rumors of the monument protections being reduced. This is no place for an oil rig or new uranium mine. This place was set aside for the remnants of the people who once called it home and the tribes who still consider this land sacred—the Hopi, Ute, Ute Mountain Ute, Navajo, Pueblo of Zuni (and dozens more).

Bears Ears is not a manicured park filled with signs, tour guides, paved roads, and obvious places for sightseeing.

For hikers, Bears Ears is an exceptional launching place for a real wilderness experience, a cultural education, and a portal into the past—the monument is considered one of the most dense with cultural sites anywhere in the U.S. Hikers must be prepared for few groomed trails, inconsistent cell phone service, zero concession stands, and no running water beyond the natural variety. Most hikes give way to scrambling over slickrock ledges and bushwhacking through densely overgrown washes.

Bears Ears requires route finding, constant attention to weather patterns, and navigating treacherous terrain. But it rewards with indelible silence and the sight of countless stars in the night sky. As you slide across quicksand alongside toads beneath desert towers and canyon walls inscribed with ancient rock art, the cacti will puncture your skin and the sand will find every orifice. Here, the desert permeates all—the wilderness is quick to reclaim all that belongs to it.

Between completing this book and the final printing, Bears Ears National Monument was reduced by 85%. Lawsuits immediately ensued, as conservation and indigenous groups petition against the illegality of the cuts. Many people asked if that meant I'd give up writing this guidebook or start over. Of course I did not, and the reduction of the monument only inspired me to continue advocating for its restored protections. It is my hope that this little book can help you learn about the bigger picture—past, present, future—of Bears Ears. Though the decision-making is largely out of public hands, the more folks like yourself who are invested in its restoration, preservation, and protection is of tremendous value. Long-distance hiking, writing books, and activism all require endurance—a dose of which I am hopeful will be used for yet another revision of this book if protections are restored.

ACKNOWLEDGMENTS

It takes the help of many people for one person to take on a project like this....

Steve and Cynthia Sjogren are the raddest parents in the world. They never questioned my choice to quit my job to become a dirty desert rat writing stories and running wild. The same goes for my Aunty Kristy and Uncle Bill Parr whose lifelong Jeep adventures inspired my lifestyle.

Thank you to the Colorado Mountain Club for supporting and publishing this labor of love. The efforts of Clyde Soles and Jodi Jennings pushed the first edition to press at rapid speed. For the second printing, it was a pleasure to work with CMC Press publisher and editor Jeff Golden.

Ralph "R. E." Burrillo and I met randomly at a coffee shop in Dolores, CO on a random day off from our lives in Bears Ears. Despite saying he'd never help with a guidebook, Ralph believed in the vision of this one and served as my research advisor. I am grateful to have a friend and comrade who loves Bears Ears as much as I do. His archaeological efforts and work with the tribes will no doubt help shape public lands policy in Bears Ears and impact the future of U.S. archaeology.

While I joyfully took on many of these routes solo, it was a pleasure to share the awe of this incredible landscape alongside Michael Versteeg and Herschel, a scrappy rez dog. Herschel sadly passed on shortly after completing this book, and these pages hold indelible memories of the places his paws explored—more than most humans.

For this second printing I added a new route, Arch Canyon, which features photos of Phil, a husky mutt (and an archae-ologist in a past-life). I met Phil and my partner Steve Eginoire (Phil's dog-father) in Bears Ears, and I am so grateful for their love and support.

Much love to my dear friends who encouraged me along the way and sent messages asking if I was still alive. And lastly, thank you for choosing me as your guide to Bears Ears. Now, do me a favor and take this book OUTSIDE!

Using This Guidebook

For some, day hikes will be enough of a challenge (see Hazards and Safety Precautions). Routefinding is necessary for almost every hike listed in this book, and while many routes are suitable for beginners, Bears Ears' routes generally demand that hikers have plenty of experience in navigation and desert and canyon travel, including reading weather patterns and sourcing water. More experienced hikers may consider this a starter guide.

Since there are few defined trails, the mileage estimates for hikes may not be exact. Likewise, the elevation change—a combination of both gain and descent—is approximate.

Use the hikes to locate the primary trailheads and build your trips from there. While this guide provides directions and maps, be sure to research routes ahead of your trip and bring along a topographical (topo) map. Visit www.fs.fed.us/visit/bears-ears-national-monument for more information.

If you have an affinity for multi-sports, fastpacking, packrafting, canyoneering, bike-packing, skiing, climbing, or

While researching this book, I lived in my Jeep within the boundaries of Bears Ears National Monument.

hunting, don't let these routes limit you. Bears Ears teems with potential adventures. You can return again and again for a constantly evolving perspective and experience.

A note about scrambling: Do not ever attempt to climb up anything that you are not certain you can also get back down the same way. If you are at all uncomfortable with a route, it is always best to turn around.

The authority for the National Monument designation is the Antiquities Act, which protects the archaeological sites and sacred tribal areas within Bears Ears' boundaries. Many of the hikes pass by or through these sensitive areas, which offer a beautiful, humbling, and critical look into the past. Please read and follow the guidance in **Respect Bears Ears**. And enjoy the historical data, anecdotes, and descriptions throughout this guidebook to enrich your hikes.

It is my hope that this guide will help you avoid driving, running, or hiking in circles and allow you to fast-forward to the action awaiting you in this spectacular and sacred landscape.

There are many rock solid reasons to visit, love, and protect Bears Ears National Monument.

Hiking Essentials

While not an exhaustive gear checklist, be sure to bring the following on every hike in Bears Ears National Monument:

1. **Navigation**—In addition to this guidebook always bring a topo map and compass. Do familiarize yourself with how to use them ahead of time. GPS and other modern navigation tools may not work without cell reception or in tight canyons, nor will their charge or battery power last for the duration

   Your cell phone won't help you here—real maps are a must!

   of many routes. Lastly, do as much research as possible about your route before your trip.

2. **Water and Filtration System**—While natural water sources exist in many places in Bears Ears, this is certainly not a lush oasis. Always bring plenty of water for before, during, and after your hikes (there is no running water or concessions within the monument). A water filtration and treatment system is a must if you plan to drink from any creeks, streams, or springs.

3. **First Aid Supplies**—In case of an emergency you will be your first source of treatment in this remote region. A basic first aid kit should include: antiseptic wipes, antibacterial ointment (e.g., bacitracin), adhesive bandages, butterfly bandages/adhesive wound-closure strips, gauze pads, non-stick sterile pads, medical adhesive tape, blister treatment, Ibuprofen/other pain-relief medication, insect sting relief treatment, antihistamine to treat allergic reactions, splinter (fine-point) tweezers, and safety pins.

4. **Sun Protection**—Sunscreen, sunglasses, and loose layers of clothing will protect you from sunburn and heat related illnesses. This is important year-round for the extreme and varied shifts in weather and temperatures in Bears Ears.

5. **Insulation**—Always bring a light jacket (at very least). This is important even during the warmest months of the year as temperatures can drop drastically at night. One of the most common causes of death in the desert is hypothermia!

6. **Extra Fuel**—A good stash of snacks with high caloric density are just as important for safety as for morale. While you can certainly splurge on fancy sports nutrition products, my favorite treats to fuel my adventures include candy bars, toaster pastries, beef jerky, nut butter, and homemade burritos. Also, be sure to lace your water with a powdered sports drink both to optimize hydration and for added energy via carbohydrates. Don't forget fuel for your vehicle too—gas stations are few and far between. It's a good idea to top off when you get a chance and even carry a spare 5 gallons.

7. **Proper Footwear**—The hikes in Bears Ears are mostly technical and on rough terrain. This is NOT the place to try and get by with sandals or ordinary sneakers. Look for a quality pair of hiking or trail running shoes with an aggressive tread. Bump up your shoe size by a half or full size to accommodate swelling. It is also recommended that you break your shoes in before your hikes to ensure that they fit properly and do not irritate your feet. As a rule, the shoe that you perceive to be most comfort-

Sole mates.

Route conditions can vary drastically, both seasonally and daily.

able (and that is designed for the given activity) will be the best shoe.

8. **Headlamp/Batteries/Fire Starter**—Sometimes hikes take longer than planned. Having a headlamp (and extra batteries) will ensure that you can navigate terrain safely in the dark. Having a fire starting option could also save your life if you do find yourself stranded overnight. Be sure to always check fire regulations and practice fire safety.

9. **Permits**—This requirement varies with each route. Permits are necessary to proceed with most overnight backcountry travel and for popular locations such as Moon House. See page 22 for more details.

10. **Positive Attitude**—A smile will go a long way—especially when the weather is hot, the snacks are melted, and the water runs dry. Preparing yourself with these essentials will improve the quality and safety of your hike, but a positive attitude is what will not only help you complete a route (if it's in the cards at all) but take back the best types of memories long after you leave.

Respect Bears Ears

"It is not enough to fight for the land; it is more important to enjoy it."   Edward Abbey

Every visit to Bears Ears National Monument must be made with a tremendous amount of respect for the land, wildlife, artifacts, indigenous history, cultural significance, and future preservation.

- **DO NOT REMOVE ARTIFACTS OR FOSSILS:** It's illegal, disrespectful, ruins the experience for others. Even moving potsherds can hinder the archaeogist's and paleontologist's ability to properly research and study the site.

- **LOOK BUT DON'T TOUCH ROCK ART:** Touching rock art can speed up the deterioration of petroglyphs and pictographs. Never alter or remove any rock art and do not grind anything in grinding stones or slicks. Lastly, do not make your own "rock art"—balanced towers and faces made from collected stones do not belong here and should be wiped away.

- **HISTORIC TRASH IS NOT TRASH:** Even things that appear to be trash like old rusty tin cans and broken bottles can provide clues about the historic period for researchers. Do not touch these items; it is illegal to remove anything over 50 years old.

- **KEEP AWAY FROM WALLS:** This includes touching, leaning, and standing on any and all historic and prehistoric structures. Some can be quite precarious and tumble at the slightest touch.

- **THIS IS NOT YOUR HOUSE:** Do not camp, start fires, eat, or go to the bathroom in or nearby archaeological remains. All can potentially cause damage, plus it's rude—no one invited you over!

- **TRAIL MARKERS:** Please do not build new cairns (rock towers marking trails). While you are likely to encounter cairns along many hikes and marking some archaeologi-

Look but do not touch!

cal sites, no additional cairns are needed to litter the landscape and view. Cairns made by hikers instead of land managers are often incorrect and can lead you astray (be careful).

- **PAD YOUR POLE:** If you use hiking poles, cover the steel point with a rubber walking tip to prevent potential damage to artifacts and rock art that may be on the ground.

- **PAY UP:** Paying permits and use fees helps with monitoring and enforcement, as well as amenities like toilets.

- **CHECK FIRE REGULATIONS:** These can vary in each area and during different times of year. Always use either a firepan or pre-existing fire rings (except those within prehistoric and historic sites), and completely extinguish the embers.

- **DON'T BUST THE CRUST:** Always stay on pre-existing trails and routes and stay off the delicate and living cryptobiotic soil—the dark brown or black clumps on the surface of sand. It can take a half century for damaged crust to regrow.

- **SOCIAL MEDIA:** It's natural to want to share photos from your trip on social media, but please refrain from referencing locations and GPS points for sensitive sites. While all routes and sites in this book are publicly available, it is best to let future explorers do their own research to guide their trip.

- **DRIVE ON OFFICIAL ROADS:** Always drive on existing roads in Bears Ears to prevent damage to the landscape and cultural sites.

- **NO ROPES:** It is illegal to use ropes and climbing gear to access archaeological sites and fragile ecosystems.

Hazards

The wilderness is not your friend! No matter how much you admire their beauty, neither desert nor mountains love you back. It is best to educate, prepare yourself, and tread with caution "in every walk with nature."

The following is an overview of the many hazards present in Bears Ears. This is not a comprehensive safety guide, but offers some fundamental suggestions. To truly ready yourself, plan your hikes according to your level of experience.

FLASH FLOODING

Flash flooding is a major concern when travelling in the canyon country, which includes the Indian Creek, Cedar Mesa, Dark Canyon, Valley of the Gods regions, and even Tuerto Canyon, high into the Abajo Mountains. Flash floods are especially common during the summer monsoon months (June through August). Flood terrain includes canyons, washes, creek beds, and low-lying desert areas.

A cloudburst can drop 4" of water in 15 minutes over a relatively small area. On a perfectly sunny day, a storm that is even 50 miles away can fill a dry canyon with 15 feet of rushing water, destroying everything in its path! It most likely will start with a bit of running water and quickly build in surges into a massive maelstrom.

A storm in the distance can mean a flash flood is rushing towards you!

To avoid this desert phenomenon, travel to these areas during the peak seasons of spring (late April to May) or fall (September and October). Regardless of the time of year, be prepared, remain aware of the weather and keep these precautions in mind:

- If thunderstorms are forecast, do not enter the canyons.
- If you see thunderstorm forming, do not enter the canyons.

If you find yourself caught in a canyon during a storm or flash flood, seek higher ground immediately. A good rule of thumb is to go twice as high as you feel you need to be to avoid the rushing water. Observe closely the watermarks along canyon walls from previous flooding. If you are camping in a canyon, be sure to set up above the watermark, preferably with a safe path to move to higher ground if needed.

NAVIGATION

Most of the routes included in this guidebook are NOT marked. In wilderness areas, trails are NOT maintained. There are no signposts (if they ever existed, many have been destroyed by weather, cattle, and people). Cairns can be misleading, and often there will be no one else on the routes to ask for directions (to the extent you dare trust the knowledge of strangers).

In addition to this guidebook, hikers must carry and know how to use a compass and a topo map. Map suggestions are provided for each route based on pre-monument regions. At present no consolidated topo map for the entire Bears Ears National Monument exists. When considering use of GPS or a smart phone with a fancy map app—please understand their limitations in an area without cell service and with routes that will often outlast a typical device battery.

TECHNICAL AND TREACHEROUS TERRAIN

Bears Ears terrain is technical and treacherous, ranging from 11,000-foot peaks to lower elevation sandy washes and rocky canyons that require Class 3 scrambling. It is believed that ancient Puebloans built their homes into the cliff walls for this very reason, for protection from enemies and weather conditions.

Please note that it is illegal to "rope up" or use technical gear to access ruins or artifacts. For the modern hiker, the opportunity for challenge and adventure is a major part of the appeal to explore this region, but it is also essential that hikers know their limits and skills before setting off on any routes.

Many of the routes listed in this guide include a variety of treacherous terrain: cliffs, steep slickrock slabs and ledges, high exposure, boulder fields, thick thorny brush, fallen trees, uneven rocky ground, baby heads (melon-sized rounded boulders in creek beds), cacti, quicksand, slick mud, water crossings, pourovers, dryfalls, sand, and more often than not, a combination of all of these obstacles at once.

Read the route descriptions carefully and do not attempt any routes featuring terrain that you are not experienced and comfortable with. For those unaccustomed to desert terrain, specifically in eastern Utah, there are plenty of easy day hikes to practice on. If you attempt moderate to difficult hikes, always do so prepared and with the mindset to confront each "obstacle" with a calculated and controlled attitude. And always be ready to retreat if any terrain proves too dangerous or you are uncertain that you can proceed safely.

DEHYDRATION/HEAT STROKE

With elevations ranging from 11,000-foot peaks to deep canyons dropping to 3,000 feet, the weather in Bears Ears can vary wildly, not only from season to season but also day to day. Winter weather can include freezing temperatures and substantial snow (especially in the higher elevations of Cedar Mesa and the Abajo Mountains) while in the lower canyons temperatures can reach above 100°F. Heatstroke and hypothermia are both concerns, and at certain times of year, for example March, are a dual hazard.

20 miles into Fable Valley, we are finally greeted with a few drops of water.

To prevent heatstroke, stay well hydrated. Always carry plenty of water and a water filter or water treatment, and know where to find water sources (and where they are lacking) on each route. Use sunscreen and reapply often, seek shade to cool off frequently, start early in the day when temperatures are cooler, pace yourself (starting slowly will prevent over-exertion and over-heating), dunk articles of clothing in cool water to lower core body temperature. Always pay attention to your vitals and other signs of heatstroke: rapid heart rate, loss of sweating, red skin, throbbing headache, dizziness, rapid shallow breathing, disorientation, seizures, and unconsciousness.

HYPOTHERMIA/FROSTBITE

Succumbing to the cold (hypothermia) is one of the most common causes of death in the desert. The climate in Bears Ears, especially atop Elk Ridge and the Abajos, can drop below freezing in the winter. Keep the following in mind to prevent hypothermia and frostbite: protect your head, hands, feet, and toes (these areas lose heat fastest and are also most susceptible to damage from the cold); wear plenty of warm layers; stay hydrated (this can seem less important when it is very cold outside, but drinking water or a sports drink with electrolytes will help your body regulate its temperature); stay dry; and keep snow out of your boots. Lastly, pay attention to the following symptoms and seek help should they surface: redness and a stinging, burning, throbbing, or prickling sensation followed by numbness.

WILDLIFE

Bears Ears is home to an abundant and diverse array of flora and fauna. Visitors may see black bears, mule deer, elk, bighorn sheep, and desert cottontails. In one typical week I crossed paths with a baby bear cub, woke up cuddling with a skunk at my bivy, uncovered a scorpion in my breakfast, and avoided a rattlesnake in a canyon. To protect yourself and wildlife please keep the following in mind:

- DO NOT TOUCH WILDLIFE
- DO NOT FEED WILDLIFE
- DO NOT REMOVE PLANTS OR WILDLIFE

Some wildlife and plant life that require special attention and precautions for visitors include, but are not limited to:

Biting flies: These are most prevalent from May to mid-to-late summer, especially in the Cedar Mesa region.

Rattlesnakes: Most active from spring to fall; be extra cautious at dawn and dusk, especially in dry washes!

Scorpions: Because they are poisonous, it is best to keep your distance! They are most active at night and love to hide in places like shoes. A high-powered LED flashlight equipped with a UV head (385 nM or less) is ideal for spotting scorpions at night.

Black bears: Although they typically avoid confrontation with humans, black bears can easily kill you. If you do encounter a bear, do not approach it and do not run—it is best to slowly move away and change directions.

Mountain lions: Mountain lions have become increasingly rare with their removal from grazing pastures over the last century. An encounter with one should be regarded as rare and special. Most attacks occur as a result of the cat mistaking you for prey, so if you do encounter one make yourself appear larger, shout, and create lots of noise.

Elk: As herd animals, it is unlikely that you will get very close, but in the event of an animal being cornered or snuck up on, they have been known to trample and maim both hikers, hunters, and pets. Always keep a distance from these massive ungulates.

Spiders, ants, bees, and centipedes: They are everywhere. You are in their kingdom.

Cacti and thorny plants: Ouch! Wearing long pants will help protect your skin from irritation and punctures.

Poison oak: Be careful near damp places and water sources.

Barrel cactus in bloom.

Remember even the most adorable wildlife and beautiful plants can cause you harm. With that in mind, do your homework ahead of time, leave the wildlife alone (no, they don't need any of your snacks), and enjoy their presence from afar.

CALLING FOR HELP

Bears Ears is truly a wilderness area with limited cellphone reception. While this provides a beautiful respite from the constant connectedness of modern society, it also presents many challenges for emergency response.

Calling for help will NOT always be possible. The nearest towns with medical assistance are Bluff, Blanding, Monticello, and Moab. In some areas of Bears Ears, these can be several hours away. Keep this in mind when planning your trip and be sure to keep your activities within your skill level.

Always tell someone where you are going before each hike. A SPOT device is a worthwhile consideration, but again it may not always have reception in deep and narrow canyon areas. Your best emergency contacts are:

BLM Monticello Field Office
365 North Main
Monticello, UT 84535
(435) 587-1500
utmtmail@blm.gov

BLM Kane Gulch Ranger Station
UT-261 (four miles south of UT-95)
Open part of the year

San Juan County Sheriff
PO Box 788
Monticello, UT 84535
(435) 587-2237
reldredge@sanjuancounty.org

DOGS AND CHILDREN

Bears Ears can be a paradise for furry four-legged companions but also poses many dangers to them. During the hottest months carry plentiful water for your dog and opt to hike only during cooler times of day to protect them from overheating and heatstroke. In many areas pets are not allowed, including

Herschel demonstrates proper hiking attire.

Grand Gulch and its tributaries, Slickhorn Canyon, Moon House Ruin, and McLoyd Canyon.

Likewise, there are few things more gleeful than watching a gaggle of sand-covered children running wild around the desert. The opportunity to explore and learn about the world around them directly goes far beyond anything they can read about in a classroom and can instill a lifelong passion for the wilderness and an active lifestyle. That said, know your children's limits, keep a close eye on them, and educate them to protect sensitive areas and stay alert in the face of natural dangers.

Permits

The permitting and fee system in Bears Ears National Monument changes frequently, varies canyon to canyon, and may continue to do so until management and monument designation issues are settled. Below is an update as of 2020, but it is advised to always read posted signs and check in with the BLM rangers for updated information and fees.

Grand Gulch, Slickhorn Canyon, canyons of Cedar Mesa, and Butler Wash require a permit for day hikes and overnight travel. Daily fees are paid at the trailhead—$5 per person or $10 per week. Consider an annual pass that covers everyone in the vehicle for $40. Overnight backpacking permits are $15 per person. Reservations can be made in advance at www.recreation.gov ($6 reservation fee applies).

To obtain unreserved/day of use permits, visit the Kane Gulch Ranger Station, which is open 8 a.m. until noon from March 1 through June 15, and September 1 through October 31. Only 20 permits are available each day for Moon House/McLoyd Canyon.

Prehistory and Archaeology

Rising from the center of the southeastern Utah landscape and visible from every direction are twin buttes so distinctive that in each of the native languages of the region their name is the same, 'Bears Ears.' For hundreds of generations, native peoples lived in the surrounding deep sandstone canyons, desert mesas, and meadow mountaintops, which constitute one of the densest and most significant cultural landscapes in the United States. Abundant rock art, ancient cliff dwellings, ceremonial sites, and countless other artifacts provide an extraordinary archaeological and cultural record that is important to us all, but most notably the land is profoundly sacred to many Native American tribes.

President Obama gave this eloquent description of Bears Ears in his December 2016 proclamation declaring its 1.35 million acres a National Monument. While he certainly paints a portrait of great beauty, an attractive tract of land in of itself is not enough to justify a National Monument designation. It is also

Many tread here before us, and many will follow after our footprints are gone. What will our legacy be?

of great scientific value with an abundance of fossils dating between 150- and 300-million years old.

The density and significance of the cultural landscape and the historical significance of Bears Ears led to its designation as a National Monument, which signifies one of the highest levels of protections for public lands. It is estimated that over 100,000 cultural sites and artifacts exist within Bears Ears National Monument, many of which hold significance for Native American tribes, along with specific geographical locations and herbs and plants that featured in sacred rituals.

For archaeologists, Bears Ears is a critical place to uncover and learn about human prehistory dating back at least 12,000 years BP (Before Present). In 1880, Charles Lang marked his name on the canyon walls and became the first person to make an officially recorded "collection" from Bears Ears. Fortunately, methods of study have evolved, but the need for more research to better understand the prehistory of the area certainly has not waned.

According to archaeologist R.E. Burrillo, in a November 2017 article for *The SAA Archaeological Record*, "Decades of research in the Bears Ears area has revealed a mosaic of human prehistory that includes populations articulating differently with different landforms depending upon time, ecology, and climate." The following is Burrillo's summary of the periods of prehistory during which humans inhabited (and migrated in and out of) the region, leaving behind remnants of their lifestyles among the canyons and mountains and in the dirt underfoot:

The Paleoindian era (ca. 12,000 to 10,000 BP) was dominated by small groups of relatively mobile foragers who used most sites only briefly or infrequently. Now-extinct Pleistocene "megafauna" (literally giant animals) were abundant on the Colorado Plateau at the time, and included saber-toothed cats, several species of horse, large-headed llama, gigantic short-faced bears, musk-ox, and woolly mammoths. While traditionally cast as obligate big-game hunters, Paleoindian foragers relied on a wide array of resources, although hunting definitely played a central role.

The Archaic era spans approximately 10,000 to 2,500 years BP, or between the end of the Paleoindian era and the appearance of agriculture, and is typically divided into Early, Middle, and Late sub-phases. The Early Archaic was a period of expanding diet, marked by increases of mean temperature and general aridity, with corresponding changes in vegetation and animal populations. Foragers began to take a broader view of "food." The Middle and Late Archaic are generally considered times of mobility, as continued environmental changes reconfigured the spatial and temporal distribution of foodstuffs.

The Formative era in the Southwest is typically sub-divided into Basketmaker II (1500 BC to AD 500), Basketmaker III (AD 500–750), Pueblo I (AD 750–900), Pueblo II (AD 900–1100), Pueblo III (AD 1100–1300), and Pueblo IV or Modern Pueblo thereafter. During these time periods, the aforementioned "mosaic" nature of human-environment interaction comes into clearest view in the culture history of Bears Ears.

The Basketmaker II period is marked by an increasingly seden-

tary settlement system, the advent of more substantial domestic dwellings, and an increasing reliance on domesticated corn and squash. Although hunting and gathering continued, there was a steady shift toward a more sedentary lifestyle until year-round settlement in loose clusters of small habitations replaced the nomadism of the Archaic period altogether. This is at least partly due to the fact that increased reliance on cultivated vegetables meant that people couldn't

Intricate pottery sherds.

leave their crops unat-
tended for too long.

The Basketmaker III period
is generally distinguished
from the preceding period
by the introduction of
three new cultural traits—
bows, beans, and ceram-
ics—all of which imply
an even more settled and
sedentary way of life. Generally, a large population
increase occurred during

Basketmaker III rock art at
Procession Panel.

this period, and leading researchers characterize it as a period
of "homesteading." In the Bears Ears area, Basketmaker III
archaeology is very well-represented east of Cedar Mesa
around Montezuma Creek and Comb Wash, and a wealth of
late-Basketmaker/early-Pueblo sites also occurs in the higher-
elevation drainages around Elk Ridge to the north, all of which
underscores the idea that this was a period of exploring and
settling new territories. Additionally, Comb Ridge's iconic Procession Panel has been interpreted as Basketmaker III rock art
depicting congregation of a large population in a central place,
signaling experiments with larger and more complex community organization preceding the transition to Pueblo I.

The Pueblo I period was one of tremendous variability and
tumultuousness throughout the Four Corners. It included many
architectural and community-level changes from the preceding
period, most notably the beginnings of full-scale villages. In
Bears Ears, all of Cedar Mesa and most of the lower-elevation
landforms in general saw drawdowns of occupation that in
some places precipitated full-on abandonment. Meanwhile,
the high-uplands area of Elk Ridge and the upper portions of
nearby drainages experienced a concomitant boom during the

Pueblo I period that compliments the depopulation noted in the surrounding areas. Originally thought to represent temporary or seasonal refuges for low-landers, it is now thought that Pueblo I populations stayed there for many generations, building some of the area's earliest village communities in the process.

The Pueblo II period is one of major demographic shifts. Around A.D. 890, a climatic change to cooler, drier conditions seems to have caused a shift in settlement patterns, and by the beginning of Pueblo II many people had moved out of the San Juan Drainage as a whole. During the AD 1000s, the climate shifted again to prevailingly hospitable conditions, with predictable growing seasons and reliable precipitation. Owing at least partly to this, the Pueblo II period saw the emergence of the "great house" system of community organization, best known and expressed in the Chaco Canyon area of northern New Mexico. The climatic plenitude of the mid-Pueblo II period accompanied a significant population surge in the Bears Ears area suggestive of immigration, possibly including the return of families who earlier had moved south to Chaco and other regions. This is supported by re-occupation of earlier Basketmaker sites by people associated with the Pueblo II period, especially on Cedar Mesa, suggesting re-occupation of the area by people who already knew it.

The bountiful rains of the early Pueblo II period meant that populations had expanded to or even passed average-year carrying capacity for local environments, putting them in a precarious position should the weather turn nasty again. Thus, when a massive drought occurred in the mid-1100s, the Chaco system fell apart and people came flooding back into the

A Pueblo III cliff dwelling.

Bears Ears area, causing a great deal more reoccupation.

A granary structure.

The Pueblo III period would be the final period of occupation for the Bears Ears area prior to the total depopulation by the AD 1270s. The locations and sizes of major settlements changed dramatically: whereas in the mid- to late-Pueblo II period most families were living on mesa tops near the best soils for farming, by the mid-Pueblo III period they had relocated their settlements nearer to reliable water sources and into canyons or cliff walls. The iconic "cliff dwellings" of Cedar Mesa and Mesa Verde alike both date to this period. Settlements often aggregated around springs and canyon heads, in a defensive gesture correlated with intergroup tensions and warfare that popped up throughout the San Juan Drainage.

These types of dwellings and storage structures can be seen on many of the hikes throughout this book including the Moon House Ruin, Perfect Kiva, and the Citadel.

It's also during the Pueblo III period that Bears Ears populations dispersed and settled the widest array of landforms, including Fable Valley, and Beef Basin—the latter of which includes such arresting examples of free-standing architecture that a portion of it is actually named Ruin Park. Towers also became common throughout the area, especially at the heads of canyons, and are thought by some researchers to be socially symbolic rather than utilitarian in nature.

Perhaps the most widely debated and discussed topic related to the Ancestoral Pueblo people is what happened to them. By the end of the AD 1200s, they were all completely gone from the area now known as Bears Ears.

However, the disappearance of the Ancestral Pueblo certainly did not signal complete depopulation of the area forever, as evidenced by the presence of Hopi ceramics and historic Pueblo shrines throughout the Bears Ears region. These indicate continued pilgrimage to the area by Pueblo peoples more-or-less continuously right up to the present day.

Meanwhile, by at least the AD 1600s—and probably well before then—Ute, Paiute, and Navajo people had taken up residence throughout the Bears Ears area, making use of the landscape and its resources in their own respective ways. Historic Navajo hogans and Ute tipi rings, along with petroglyphs associated with both cultures, can be found throughout the area.

The twin sandstone formations of the Bears Ears themselves figure prominently in cultural narratives, and traditional practices like the gathering of firewood and medicinal plants continue there to this day. In fact, over 20 tribes throughout the region regard the Bears Ears as an important part of their sacred geography, which underscores the importance of visiting the place with respect.

Modern Times

In modern history, perhaps no event is more significant to Bears Ears and the surrounding towns of Bluff, Blanding, and Monticello than the San Juan Expedition, known more commonly as the "Hole-in-the-Rock Expedition." The expedition was sent by the Mormon Church to establish a settlement on the San Juan River in order to foster trade and relationships with the Navajo to the south.

The journey began in 1879, a year that experienced a harsh winter, which made it extremely difficult for the outfit 250 people, 83 wagons, and over 1,000 head of livestock. They had to traverse difficult terrain that included canyons with

Sunset alpenglow on the west butte of Bears Ears.

sandstone cliffs, sandy ravines, mud that sucked wagon wheels into the earth, and unforgiving mountains dense with forests.

The pioneers used dynamite to blast an actual "hole" into the sandstone above the Colorado River, in present day Glen Canyon National Recreation Area, to precariously allow passage through the area. When they reached present-day Bears Ears, they climbed Salvation Knoll to get their bearings. Triangulating their location based on the Blue Mountains (now known as the Abajos), they were able to guide their wagon train due east. Amazingly, no one was seriously injured or killed and they eventually settled near the San Juan River forming the town of Bluff.

Monument Background

In 1906, Congress passed the Antiquities Act, which gave the President authorization to designate lands owned by the government that contained "historic landmarks, historic and prehistoric structures, and other objects of historic or scientific interest" as national monuments. To date, 16 presidents from both parties have used their authority to designate 157 national monuments; 54 of these were over 85,000 acres. Congress later upgraded 38 monuments to national park status for additional protection.

The United States government took possession of Utah after the Mexican War of 1848. Utah was initially a Territory before it finally became a state in 1896. Suffice to say, there were some troubles between Mormon settlers and the U.S. government.

Starting in 1869, the U.S. Government Land Office (GLO) managed the land that currently makes up the **Bears Ears National Monument** (BENM) and pretty much all of Utah. In 1907, a portion of the area near Monticello was transferred to the Forest Service (USFS) for what is now called the **La Sal-Manti National Forest**. Some of the region fell under control of the Grazing Service in 1934, which eventually merged with the GLO in 1946 to become the Bureau of Land Management (BLM).

Neighboring **Canyonlands National Park** came into existence in 1964, covering 330,000 acres; the only one of Utah's "Big 5" national parks that did not begin as a monument. In 1972, Congress established the 1.25-million-acre **Glen Canyon National Recreation Area** largely for access to Lake Powell after completion of the Glen Canyon Dam in 1966; it is administered by the National Park Service (NPS).

The 7,300-acre **Natural Bridges National Monument** became Utah's first in 1908; it is administered by the NPS. In 1974, the BLM designated the 33,000-acre **Grand Gulch Primitive Area** and the 62,000-acre **Dark Canyon Primitive Area** (lower part). The Utah Wilderness Act of 1984 created 47,000-acre **Dark Canyon Wilderness** (upper part), which is managed by the USFS.

In 1976, Congress mandated the BLM to inventory roadless areas and designate potential Wilderness Study Areas (WSA). These lands don't receive full wilderness protection but must be managed with that in mind. It takes an act of Congress to either elevate WSAs to wilderness areas or to remove their status. In BENM, there are over 380,000 acres of WSA, including: Bridger Jack Mesa, Butler Wash, Cedar Mesa, Mancos Mesa, and Mule Canyon.

The USFS also administers almost 90,000 acres based on the 2001 Roadless Rule. And the BLM manages around 50,000 acres, like the Valley of the Gods, as Areas of Critical Environmental Concern. Both of these designations can be revoked without approval from Congress.

Complicating jurisdiction, the state of Utah owns over 109,000 acres split between 140 plots within BENM. Known as "trust lands," these were granted upon statehood to serve as a permanent trust for schools. An additional 12,600 acres is private property. This non-Federal land is not in the monument and can only voluntarily be purchased or traded; a land swap takes years of negotiation.

Monument Status

On December 28th 2016, President Obama created **Bears Ears National Monument**. That action resulted from many years of research and consultation with the local community. By contrast, the **Grand Staircase-Escalante National Monument**, created by President

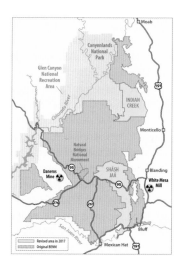

Clinton in 1996, was a surprise announcement intended to block a proposed coalmine; the failure to consult with interested parties still reverberates.

In 2015, after six years of effort, the Bears Ears Inter-Tribal Coalition consisting of five tribes (Hopi, Ute, Ute Mountain Ute, Navajo, and Pueblo of Zuni) proposed a 1.9 million-acre national monument. In an attempt to appease any opposition, Obama reduced the monument to

1.35 million acres. In particular, BENM left out the Daneros uranium mine and oil fields in the Comb Ridge area.

Five months prior to Obama's declaration, two Utah congressmen introduced legislation for the Public Lands Initiative (PLI) that offered land-use planning for 1.3 million acres of the region. About 86% of the land in Bears Ears National Monument was proposed in the PLI and only 8% of the land in the PLI was left out. Billed as a "grand bargain" resulting from three years of discussions, the PLI was a far-reaching proposal that covered much of eastern Utah. When the bill failed to make it out of committee, Obama had little time to act before his term ended.

The national monument designation shifted BLM and USFS priorities from multiple uses, to protection of resources. Cattle grazing, timber harvesting, and hunting are still allowed and the entire area is open to everyone; off-road vehicles must use existing roads and designated trails. The main restrictions are creations of new roads and extraction of minerals and petroleum, which is what much of the current fuss is about.

Deposits of uranium exist, arcing from the western edge near Mancos Mesa up through Lockhart Basin, as well as around Comb Ridge. In addition, Lockhart Basin and Indian Creek contain potash (a potassium salt used for fertilizer) as well as oil and gas deposits. A relatively small area of tar sands lies in BENM as well. Petroleum also exists in the southeast corner between Blanding and Bluff. At present, none of these resources are economically viable.

All hikes in this book, regardless of monument status, remain on public lands.

On December 4th, 2017 President Trump proclaimed a reduction of the size of BENM by 85%. Until courts decide otherwise, it will now become two monuments: Shash Jáa ("Bears Ears" in Navajo) at roughly 130,000 acres and Indian Creek at almost 72,000 acres. Shash Jáa includes the Bears Ears buttes as well as parts of Arch and Mule Canyons.

There is precedent for this reduction. In 1915, Woodrow Wilson diminished Mount Olympus National Monument by 313,000 acres, reducing it by almost half. And 25 years later, Franklin Roosevelt reduced part of Grand Canyon National Monument by almost 72,000 acres to allow for cattle ranching. Until BENM, no President has excised part of a monument since 1963.

However, it remains unclear whether a President has the authority to revoke or reduce a national monument. In the Forest Service Organic Act of 1897, Congress specifically gave the President the power to modify or revoke the designation of a national forest. Nine years later, when the Antiquities Act passed, there was no mention of such an authorization. Yet one of the provisions states that the President should preserve "the smallest area compatible with the proper care and management of the objects to be protected."

It will take years of litigation to resolve the status of BENM, most likely with a decision from the U.S. Supreme Court. The stakes are much higher than this one monument; the outcome will affect dozens of national monuments and millions of acres around the country.

In the meantime, current Federal law protects all of the hikes in this book. In addition to Shásh Jaá and Indian Creek National Monuments, the Dark Canyon Wilderness remains for the ages. All of the WSAs will retain their status without an act of Congress. Combined, that's around 600,000 acres that are off limits to development. The rest of the area within BENM has weaker protection but is still under the control of the BLM and USFS.

Regional Overview

It certainly is possible to visit more than one region during a trip to Bears Ears, but it will require significant car travel. Each area teems with its own distinct details, routes, and conditions. In writing this guide, I experienced all four seasons in Bears Ears while watching conditions change and immersing myself in each unique world.

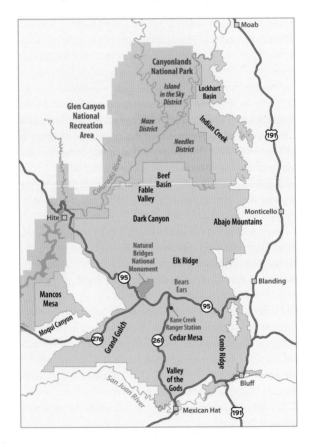

When the heat intensified in the desert canyons, I simply drove high up on Elk Ridge to enjoy the cool breezes at 8,000-feet elevation, while a cold snap with snow flurries in the high country of the Abajos sent me back down to seek out an elusive swimming hole in considerably warmer temperatures of the canyons. My total immersion in Bears Ears taught me above all that even a lifetime of exploration here would leave areas unseen.

Deciding which area to visit may be the most challenging part of any trip to Bears Ears and, for the highly curious, one trip will undoubtedly inspire return visits. I recommend spending at least one full day in each region or, ideally, several days devoted to multiple routes in a localized area.

ELK RIDGE AND DARK CANYON

Elk Ridge is home to the actual "Bears Ears," the two wingate sandstone formations rising to 8,929 and 9,058 feet for which the monument is named. Every indigenous tribe that holds them sacred uses some variation of this term—Shash Jah means Bears Ears in Diné. The area is characterized by mountainous high-elevation terrain dotted with ponderosa pines. The plateau reaches 9,000 feet in some areas with dramatic drops as much as 1,200 feet from trailheads like Woodenshoe or Peavine Canyons into Dark Canyon.

Elk Ridge

In Dark Canyon, sandstone and limestone layered walls and natural arches tower overhead and trails meander in and out of piñon-juniper woodlands, eventually descending into blackbrush and sagebrush at lower elevations. In general, the wooded higher elevation of upper Dark Canyon tends to be dry (in terms of creek beds and water sources) for most of the year, while lower Dark Canyon features year-round water running through pour-offs, waterfalls, and pools. Elk Ridge and Dark Canyon may be inaccessible during winter months due to snow. Be prepared at any time of year for extreme and varied temperatures and weather reflecting this dramatic and diverse region.

HIKES: *Dark Canyon and its tributaries (Woodenshoe Canyon and Peavine Canyon), Scorup Cabin, and Hammond Canyon.*

CEDAR MESA AND GRAND GULCH

Cedar Mesa is the heart of Bears Ears National Monument and Grand Gulch is its bona fide crown jewel. It is dense with cultural sites reflecting the habitation of Ancestoral Puebloans and other native peoples who migrated in and out of the area. Sitting on a plateau averaging 4,200 feet elevation (6,500 at its highest, where large weather swings occur) but lined with canyons diving over 1,000 feet further below, the climate of Cedar Mesa can be harsh. Spring and fall are ideal times for visiting this area. Winter temperatures can drop below freezing with canyon walls and entrance points icing over, and summer temperatures can top 100°F. Flash floods are a risk in monsoon season, which lasts from early July until September.

HIKES: *House On Fire Ruin, Moon House Ruin, the Citadel, Road Canyon, Grand Gulch and Tributaries (Toadie Canyon, Kane Gulch, Bullet Canyon, Sheiks Canyon), Slickhorn Canyon, and Fish Canyon/Owl Canyon Loop.*

COMB RIDGE AND BUTLER WASH

Comb Ridge is a sandstone monocline over 80 miles long originating in Kayenta, Arizona, and ending in Blanding, Utah, near the Abajo Mountains. The formation spans Bears Ears National Monument, and jutting vertically 300 to 900 feet into the horizon, can be clearly viewed from nearly every high point in Cedar Mesa, Elk Ridge, and the Abajo Mountains. Comb Ridge features many canyon clefts used by Ancient Puebloans as protection from the elements and probably enemies as well. Evidence of this use can be seen on many hikes featured in this

Comb Ridge

book such as those to Procession Panel and Wolfman Panel. The base of Comb Ridge and the areas it passes through, like the shallow Butler Wash drainage on Comb Ridge's east side, are notoriously hot in the summer months, making spring and fall an ideal time for a trip here.

HIKES: *Arch Canyon, Wolfman Panel and Small Ruin, Procession Panel, and Monarch Cave.*

FABLE VALLEY AND BEEF BASIN

Connecting the Dark Canyon plateau with Beef Basin, Fable Valley is a gentle canyon, albeit one of the most remote in Bears Ears. The Fable Valley hiking route was originally used by four-wheel-drive vehicles but is now closed to motor traffic. Fable Valley is an open and shallow sandstone-lined valley covered in sagebrush with a grassy floor until its confluence with Gypsum Canyon, where it dramatically drops into this stunningly deep, colorful, and lush canyon. Cattle ranchers historically used Beef Basin for grazing. Note that these areas can become quite hot and water is scarce. While it is possible to reach the Fable Valley Trailhead with two-wheel-drive, the roads to Beef Basin are rough and may require a four-wheel-drive vehicle with high clearance.

HIKES: *Fable Valley*

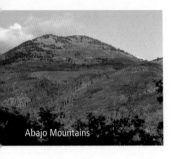
Abajo Mountains

THE ABAJO (BLUE) MOUNTAINS

Barely outside Bears Ears National Monument, Abajo Peak (11,360 feet) is adjoined by a series of several other high elevation peaks. The area is scattered with aspen and oak groves and is home to bear, deer, and elk. Panoramic views of the entire monument are available here, notably the dramatic desert towers of Indian Creek, the Bears Ears mesas, Elk Ridge, Comb Ridge, and numerous deep sandstone canyons. On a clear day you can enjoy views extending to Sleeping Ute Mountain in Colorado and Shiprock in New Mexico.

HIKES: *Skyline Trail/Tuerto Canyon Loop, Lower Indian Creek Trail.*

Indian Creek

INDIAN CREEK

Known as one of the most popular trad climbing destinations in the world, Indian Creek's high walls of deep red wingate sandstone and views of striking desert towers will delight even those who visit and remain on the ground. Situated at just over 5,000 feet, spring and fall are ideal times to travel to the area to avoid high heat and freezing temperatures common in summer and winter. The impressive Newspaper Rock petroglyph panel can be found here. The road to Indian Creek is also the entrance to the Needles District of Canyonlands National Park.

HIKES: *Lower Indian Creek Trail and Newspaper Rock.*

LOCKHART BASIN

Just south of Moab, Lockhart Basin is the northernmost part of Bears Ears and is in the heart of desert canyon country. Recreation-wise, Lockhart Basin is best known for its four-wheel-drive routes and mountain biking.

HIKES: *There are no established hiking routes in Lockhart Basin. There are several mountain bike and four-wheel-drive routes and the Hayduke Trail passes through here.*

VALLEY OF THE GODS

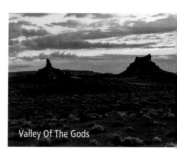
Valley Of The Gods

Often compared in beauty to the nearby Monument Valley, Valley of the Gods contains stunning desert towers, isolated buttes, and sandstone walls. Expect desert conditions in this area north of Mexican Hat, Utah.

HIKES: *There are no established hiking routes in Valley of the Gods. It is possible to hike (or run or bike) the 17-mile dirt road loop that encompasses the area.*

MOQUI CANYON/ MANCOS MESA

Moqui Canyon

When you look at a map of Bears Ears National Monument you may notice a tiny swath of land just off to the side of the main boundaries adjacent to Lake Powell and behind the Clay Hills. The area features several canyons, such as Moqui Canyon and Red Canyon, with wingate sandstone walls, sand dunes, and desert conditions.

HIKES: *No hikes from this region are included in this guide, but it is certainly possible to explore this beautiful area on foot.*

NATURAL BRIDGES NATIONAL MONUMENT

This monument within a monument is home to three huge bridges formed by rushing water (arches form by seeping moisture and frost). In 2007, the International Dark Sky Association certified it as the world's first "International Dark Sky Park."

HIKES: *All three bridges are short hikes (under 1.2 miles round-trip). The mighty Sipapu Bridge, second largest in the world, spans 268 feet while the elegant Owachomo Bridge is only 9 feet thick.*

Roadside Attractions

In addition to the hikes described in this guide, there are many worthwhile places devoid of official trails that are worth a stop during your visit for their beauty and historical significance.

RIVER HOUSE RUIN

Mormon settlers visited River House Ruin, located near the San Juan River and Sand Island, on the Hole-in-the-Rock Expedition after they climbed over Comb Ridge on their way to Bluff. Previously it was called Snake House for the pictograph on the back wall. The storage structures dating back to the Pueblo III culture (AD 1150–1260s) are thought to be one of the most thoroughly stabilized and rebuilt sites in the entire region, alongside Butler Wash Ruin.

EDGE OF THE CEDARS MUSEUM

This Blanding establishment offers an up-close look at an incredible collection of artifacts found in the Bears Ears region that includes an intact kiva (for those unable to hike to ruins to see one up close), the original ladder discovered in Slick-horn Canyon's Perfect Kiva, and an original sash adorned with bright red and blue macaw feathers!

MOKI DUGWAY

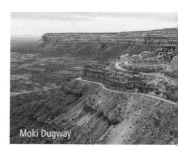
Moki Dugway

This winding dirt road is a portion of UT Highway 261, which is a common route into Bears Ears and many of the hikes in this guide, when approaching from Mexican Hat. The road is steep (11 percent grade), 3-miles long, and switchbacked. It is possible to travel here with two-wheel-drive, but this is not recommended during wet weather conditions due to slick, sticky mud.

MULEY POINT

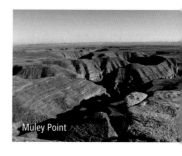
Muley Point

The first turnoff at the top of the Moki Dugway, Muley Point offers one of the best views in the region that extends to Valley of the Gods, Comb Ridge, Goose-necks State Park, Glen Canyon, and Monument Valley. At times four-wheel-drive may be required to pass through the rough road to the point.

Through Hiking

While a through-hiking route has not been designated in Bears Ears, several notable routes pass through Bears Ears National Monument. All feature historical components inspired by various outcasts who tread through Bears Ears and its surrounding area seeking refuge, escape, and solitude. In addition to the routes listed in this book, portions of these routes that cross into Bears Ears are worth considering during your visit.

THE HAYDUKE TRAIL

It's almost impossible to think about the Utah desert without referencing Edward Abbey at some point, especially his novel *The Monkey Wrench Gang*. Named after the novel's anti-hero, Hayduke, this through-hiking route covers 800 miles of eastern Utah's most striking, historical, and deadly backcountry terrain. A portion of the trek crosses through Bears Ears and includes several of the routes featured in this book: Fable Valley, Dark Canyon, and Butler Wash.

THE OUTLAW TRAIL

Running 2,000 miles from Montana to Mexico, the Outlaw Trail, which covers notoriously dangerous terrain, was used by criminals like Butch Cassidy and the Wild Bunch to move incognito across the west. Several hundred miles of the route pass through Utah, including Hideout Canyon, which is in Bears Ears.

THE HOLE-IN-THE-ROCK TRAIL

Starting in Escalante and ending in Bluff, the 180-mile Hole-in-the-Rock Trail follows the route of the Mormon pioneers who traversed the Utah desert to establish a settlement in Bluff, blasting their way through a canyon wall in what is now Lake Powell en route. You can find segments of this route passing through Bears Ears, such as at Salvation Knoll, which are marked by wooden sign posts depicting a covered wagon.

Aerial view of Valley of the Gods, the Moki Dugway, and the Goosenecks of the San Juan River. Photo by Gary Crabbe

1. House on Fire

RATING:	Easy
DISTANCE:	2 miles round-trip (Option to extend this hike up to 8 miles)
ELEVATION CHANGE:	100 feet
ROUND-TRIP TIME:	Short day hike
MAP:	Trails Illustrated Grand Gulch, Cedar Mesa Plateau
NEAREST LANDMARK:	The town of Blanding
NOTE:	Permit required

COMMENT: The photogenic House on Fire in Mule Canyon makes an excellent introductory hike to the Cedar Mesa Region of Bears Ears, with easy access from Highway 95 and a short approach. The route is flat and meanders along a partially shaded streambed that is lush and overgrown. Note that water availability from the stream varies drastically throughout the year.

The wildflowers, including barrel cactus blossoms, evening primrose, and firecracker penstemon, are exceptional during late spring. House on Fire is the remains of granaries, or basically fancy storage structures, used by the Pueblo III people to house corn and food sources during about 1150–1275. The structure is built beneath a naturally streaked sandstone overhang that appears to be ablaze with flames, especially when the light hits it just right during late morning and at sunset. Be sure to pack your camera for this hike!

GETTING THERE: From Blanding, take Highway 95 and go right on County Road 263/Texas Flat Road. Non-four-wheel-drive vehicles should park in the first lot on the left side of the road

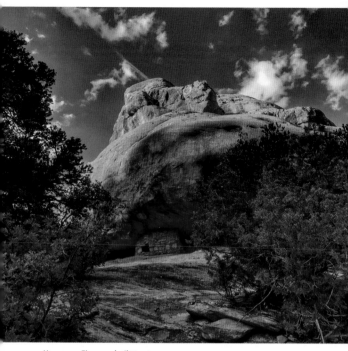

House on Fire was built to store corn.

and then walk the 0.25 mile on to the trailhead. Four-wheel-drive vehicles can continue farther and park on the roadside near the trailhead.

THE ROUTE: From the road, descend to the trailhead, which begins with a wide vegetated flat area before veering into the somewhat narrow canyon where the trail meanders along the streambed. The seasons are noticeable in this region; I found the trail and creek completely iced over in February, flowing with ample water in March, completely dried up by May, and slick with thick mud in August during monsoon season.

Springtime reflections in Mule Canyon. At other times of the year, the creek bed can be frozen over or dried up.

House On Fire.

Approximately 1 mile into the hike, you will encounter a well-worn spur trail heading toward the right hand wall of the canyon, which leads to the House on Fire. Initially the granaries are slightly obstructed from view by trees, but are visible after a couple of paces up the trail spur.

ROUTE EXTENSION: For those looking to hike longer, Mule Canyon continues for several miles, making it an approximately 8-mile out-and-back route.

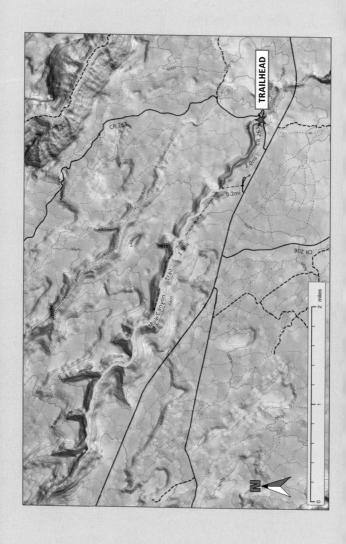

TRAILHEAD

CR 263

CR 263

1.0mi

0.2mi

1.1mi

Mule Canyon Trail

CR 236

N

0   1   2 miles

2. Moon House

RATING:	Moderate
DISTANCE:	3.2 miles round-trip; over 5 miles if you park in the first lot
ELEVATION CHANGE:	300 feet
ROUND-TRIP TIME:	Short day hike
MAP:	Trails Illustrated Grand Gulch, Cedar Mesa Plateau
NEAREST LANDMARK:	Kane Gulch Ranger Station
NOTE:	Permit required; no dogs allowed

COMMENT: Although this is a fairly short hike, you will want to give yourself ample time to explore and enjoy the Moon House Ruin. The site contains many structures,

The dramatic scenery of McLoyd Canyon.

most of which were used for storage. According to tree-ring analysis, this ruin was one of the last-occupied sites on all of Cedar Mesa, dating back to AD 1150–1260s. Consult the **Respect Bears Ears** section (page 14-15) before visiting.

A day use permit is required for this route, with only 20 allowed each day. Reserve in advance at www.recreation.gov.

A four-wheel-drive vehicle with high clearance is recommended to get to this trailhead, and depending on your comfort level driving on a rough, high-centered road, you may want to consider parking at the first dirt lot across the road from the trail kiosk. Add approximately 2 miles from here to get to the trailhead.

There is very little shade on this hike so if you are visiting during a hot time of day or year come prepared with water, sunscreen, and appropriate attire. In addition, this route climbs up and down slickrock that is marked by cairns. If you are not comfortable with Class 3 scrambling and steep downhills, or are scared of heights, consider enjoying the view of the Moon House Ruin where the traditional dirt single-track trail ends across the canyon.

GETTING THERE: From Blanding, go south on US 191 for 4.0 miles. Take a right (north) onto UT 95 and continue for 28.4 miles. Turn left (south) on UT 261 and continue for 10.1 miles (you will pass the Kane Gulch Ranger Station 6.2 miles down this road). Between mileposts 22 and 23, go left on Snow Flat Road (where the road splits) for 8.2 miles. There is a two-wheel-drive parking lot at the kiosk for anyone unable to proceed on the very rough road. If continuing to the main trailhead, go right at the kiosk and follow the unmarked dirt road for 1.2 miles until you reach the parking area.

From Mexican Hat, go north on US 163 for 3.9 miles and make a left on UT 261, which you will follow for 22.6 miles. Turn right on Snow Flat Road and then proceed with the directions above.

Original paint is still present on the walls of Moon House.

McLoyd Canyon rock art.

THE ROUTE: From the final parking lot, head down the trail marked by a crown BLM post (it says "No Motorized Vehicles Beyond This Point"). Follow this single-track path through piñon, juniper, and sagebrush for approximately 0.25 mile until you reach the rim of McLoyd Canyon. For those looking for a shorter hike or to avoid steep and rocky terrain, continue just a bit farther until the Moon House Ruin comes into view.

To proceed, carefully follow the cairns over and along the canyon ledge (this is where you will find the best view of Moon House from this side of the canyon). The route drops over 100 feet in a short amount of time via steep slickrock and requires some easy downclimbing until you reach the canyon floor.

Continue across the short canyon floor, veering right around a massive boulder that sits at the base of the last set of cairns. The next cairns will guide you upward on the other side of the canyon and directly to Moon House. Again, the first few moves up require some scrambling (possibly on all fours) to boost yourself up onto the slickrock.

From here, follow the zigzag of cairns that trend left toward the Moon House. The structures are beneath the alcove in the canyon and spread out along a quarter-mile stretch. It is possible to continue on in either direction (follow the cairns) and enjoy several other ancestral sites.

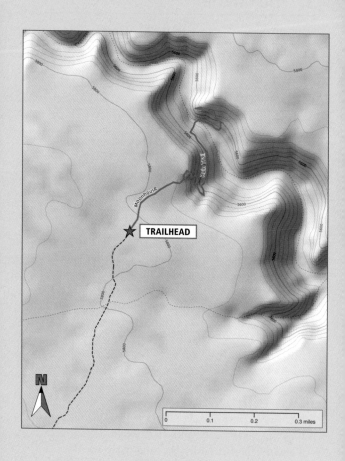

TRAILHEAD

N

0	0.1	0.2	0.3 miles

3. The Citadel

RATING:	Moderate
DISTANCE:	4.2 miles round-trip (5.7 miles if you walk from the two-wheel-drive parking lot)
ELEVATION CHANGE:	200 feet
ROUND-TRIP TIME:	Short day hike
MAP:	Trails Illustrated Grand Gulch, Cedar Mesa Plateau
NEAREST LANDMARK:	Kane Gulch Ranger Station
NOTE:	Permit required

COMMENT: The Citadel is one of the most striking structures in Bears Ears National Monument, sitting prominently atop a breathtaking natural land bridge that juts out across Road Canyon, with sweeping views of the entire area. A hike to the Citadel cannot be missed on a trip to this area and it is worth planning extra time to visit this special location.

If you like to take photographs, consider timing your outing during early morning or evening for best lighting conditions. Before hiking to this stunning and well-preserved (stabilized) site that was used by the Pueblo III culture, be sure to read the **Respect Bears Ears** section (page 14-15). Although no longer visible, two rock walls ran across the sandstone walkway leading toward The Citadel, most likely to deter invaders.

While this hike is fairly short and moderate, there are several sections of exposed slickrock that require easy Class 3 scrambling with high exposures, which could prove fatal should you fall. Anyone not experienced with travel on these surfaces should not attempt this hike. Alternatively, you may enjoy the view from the lovely first few miles of flat and well-marked single-track along the canyon rim.

Another consideration is Cigarette Springs Road, which can be extremely rough during portions of the year, and as it nears the trailhead to this route, it becomes especially unruly. If you do not have a four-wheel-drive vehicle with high clearance it is recommended that you park your car at the turnoff for the trailhead and walk the additional section of road (adding 1.5 miles round-trip to your route). Regardless of your type of vehicle, pay attention to road conditions and weather. This road can become impassable during wet or snowy weather, and with no cell phone reception or road services nearby it isn't the type of place you want to get stuck!

GETTING THERE: From Blanding, take US Highway 95 to County Road 261 and go left. Stop at the Kane Gulch Ranger Station for information, permits, and restrooms. Continue for 9.7 miles to Cigarette Springs Road, which is marked with a sign between mileposts 19 and 20, and make a left. The turn for the Citadel Trailhead is 5.4 miles down this road on the left. Once you make this left, continue on the extremely rough road for 0.75 mile to the parking area where there is a kiosk to purchase a day-use permit.

Contemplating the beauty and future of Bears Ears.

| The Citadel. | Enjoy the jaunt across the land bridge. |

From Mexican Hat, drive north on US 163 for 3.9 miles and turn left (north) on UT 261. Follow UT 261 for slightly over 19 miles and make a right turn on County Road 239 (look for the Cigarette Springs Road sign) between mileposts 20 and 19. Proceed with directions above.

THE ROUTE: From the parking area follow the cairn-marked trail east that parallels the edge of the canyon. The flat trail meanders through a beautiful juniper and piñon forest that occasionally crosses over sections of flat slickrock well-marked by cairns. At just over 1.5 miles this flat portion of trail ends and begins a descent over the canyon rim where the land bridge first comes into view. If you are not comfortable and experienced with Class 3 scrambling, slickrock, and exposure, this is where you should turn around.

To continue, follow the cairns down and onto the slickrock ledge that clearly leads to the land bridge. Opt to take the path that is most level and a safe distance from a precipitous fall off the edge and into the canyon. Once on the land bridge, continue toward the obvious rock formation at its tip. Follow the cairns and scramble up. Circumnavigate the formation for incredible views of Road Canyon and of course the Citadel itself, which is tucked just beneath the natural roof that the rock forms.

TRAILHEAD

4. Road Canyon

RATING:	Moderate
DISTANCE:	12 miles round-trip
ELEVATION CHANGE:	700 feet
ROUND-TRIP TIME:	Full-day hike or overnight
MAP:	Trails Illustrated Grand Gulch, Cedar Mesa Plateau
NEAREST LANDMARK:	Kane Gulch Ranger Station
NOTE:	Permit required

COMMENT: Road Canyon is home to several notable archaeological sites, including Fallen Roof Ruin, Ruin Viewpoint, and Seven Kivas—read **Respect Bears Ears** (page 14-15) before this hike. Most of these sites are typical of the late Pueblo (PII and/or PIII) period when people began to cluster around water sources instead of on arable mesa-top lands. Although this canyon typically offers a good source of water, it was not densely populated and was abandoned before Fish, Owl, and Arch canyons were deserted in the northeast.

Seven Kivas.

While the route covers mostly non-technical flat, sandy, and slickrock washes, the approaches to Ruin Viewpoint and beyond to Seven Kivas require some scrambling over slickrock surfaces. For those not experienced or comfortable with these types of terrain, consider another route. Always check weather conditions and be alert for flash flood warnings (see **Flash Flooding**, page 16). Despite the real dangers associated with an influx of too much water, Road Canyon can become quite dry most of the year, so plan ahead and bring plenty of water and a filtration system. Nearby hikes include The Citadel. Plan to spend at least two days near Cigarette Springs Road, if possible.

GETTING THERE: From Blanding, take US Highway 95 to County Road 261 and go left. Stop at the Kane Gulch Ranger Station for information, permits, and restrooms. Continue for 9.7 miles to Cigarette Springs Road (which is marked with a sign between mileposts 19 and 20) and make a left. Note that 0.75 mile from the paved road, there is a kiosk where you can purchase a day-use permit. Reset your odometer at the start of Cigarette Springs Road. The inconspicuous and unmarked access road is at 3.1 miles on your left. Take it and continue to the parking area where you will find trail signs.

From Mexican Hat, drive north on US 163 for 3.9 miles and turn left (north) on UT 261. Follow UT 261 for 19.1 miles and make a right turn on County Road 239 (look for the Cigarette Springs Road sign) between mileposts 20 and 19. Continue with directions as above.

THE ROUTE: From the parking area, follow the single-track trail until you approach the rim of the canyon in less than 0.5 mile. The descent into Road Canyon is gentle, over switchbacks and guided by cairns. If you intend to hike to your vehicle via this same entrance, be sure to pay attention to what this section looks like to ensure a successful return

Fallen Roof Ruin.

to the trailhead. From here, the trail follows the wash and occasionally moves adjacent to it, which may require walking through thick brush. Keep your eyes open for a sandstone pillar followed by a slickrock pour-off (walk down it). Look for cairns to the left indicating the route up along the slickrock ledge to the Fallen Roof Ruin (named for the chunks of rock that are flaking off the natural roofs of these four structures). Turn around here for a nice 3-mile round-trip hike.

For Ruin Viewpoint, continue back the way you came back down to the route that follows the canyon floor. After about 3.5 miles, you will encounter and need to bypass three pour-offs. After the third, look for a set of cairns guiding you up the slickrock bench on the side of the canyon. Continue for approximately 0.5 mile until a set of ruins across the canyon on the north wall comes into view. To descend into the canyon, either retrace your steps (which will add approximately 1 mile to this route) or seek out cairns leading down to the canyon floor.

To reach Seven Kivas, continue along the canyon, which begins to curve northward at just over 5 miles. At 5.5 miles, it redirects again, this time northeast, before veering east at 6.0 miles. Keep hiking over a wide expanse of slickrock that opens up until a set of ruins is visible along the canyon wall. Always respect the chains put up by the BLM around these fragile sites.

To return to the trailhead, retrace your steps down the canyon.

CITADEL TRAIL

TRAILHEAD

CR 239

2 miles

5. Arch Canyon

RATING:	Moderate
DISTANCE:	24 Miles
ELEVATION CHANGE:	800 Feet
ROUND-TRIP TIME:	2–5 days
MAPS:	Trails Illustrated Manti La Sal
NEAREST LANDMARK:	The town of Blanding

COMMENT: Though it's named for its three prominent arches (Cathedral Arch, Angel Arch, and Keystone Arch), this box canyon is representative of the variation and significance tucked into every corner of Bears Ears. The hike begins in a sandy wash but leads to a forest of Douglas fir, ponderosa pine, pinyon, juniper, and maple. The fantastic geological formations enshrine and protect numerous cultural sites. Please utilize the suggestions in **Respect Bears Ears** on this and all hikes. Water conditions are always variable, but the creek in Arch Canyon is a reliable source of year-round water. It is possible, with 4WD and high clearance, to bypass the first 8 miles and shorten the route. However, walking allows you to stretch your legs and your neck as you crane your head up to take in the views of the canyon's high sandstone walls, arches, and towers.

Don't forget to pause and admire the view.

GETTING THERE: From Blanding, take Highway 95 for approximately 14 miles and go right on County Road 205, Comb Wash (approximately 1 mile after you pass through Comb Ridge). Take Comb Wash for 2.5 miles to the parking area and mouth of Arch Canyon. CR 205 is a dirt road and may become impassable in wet conditions. Please note that this road is surrounded by Ute Tribal lands. Traveling off this designated road is considered trespassing.

Arch Canyon's namesake.

THE ROUTE: From the well-marked parking lot, set off down the wide Jeep/ATV road. The Arch Canyon Ruins will immediately stall your momentum, but it's worth the stop to admire this fenced cultural site (likely to protect it from the cows and ATVs that frequent this area). Though the road parallels the creek, expect several crossings (most are possible without getting wet) on this 8.5-mile stretch. There is a large primitive campsite, and several smaller spots, at the end of the ATV road, making this an ideal basecamp for overnight trips. Continue up the faint single-track path the remaining 4.5 miles of Arch Canyon, then head back the way you came for a 9-mile round-trip from camp to camp. This stretch includes the three notable arches, meanders in and out of the wash, and is shaded by towering conifers. The trail ends at a high pourover, which is possible to get around, but most hikers will use this as a turnaround point.

To extend your trip, consider hiking through Texas and/or Butts Canyon. Both contain faint primitive use trails and are done as out-and-back dayhikes from the Arch Canyon campsites.

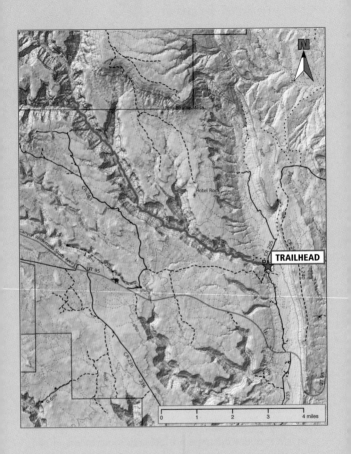

TRAILHEAD

6. Fish Canyon/ Owl Canyon Loop

RATING:	Strenuous
DISTANCE:	17 miles total
ELEVATION CHANGE:	3,000 feet
ROUND-TRIP TIME:	Overnight
MAP:	Trails Illustrated Grand Gulch, Cedar Mesa Plateau
NEAREST LANDMARK:	Kane Gulch Ranger Station
NOTE:	Permit required

COMMENT: The Fish-Owl Loop is considered a Cedar Mesa hiking classic for good reason—it links two distinct canyons that include dramatic geological features, like Natural Arch and

Looking down into Fish Canyon—Elk Ridge and Bears Ears line the horizon.

Monsoon season moisture at the bottom of Fish Canyon.

Nevills Arch. It features canyon walls that tower to 500 feet and sometimes has abundant water sources in springs and creeks. And the cultural sites located below the rim of the Owl Canyon entrance at the trailhead encapsulate the lore of visiting Bears Ears National Monument. The big site on the right as you ascend from Owl Canyon is typical of the Great Pueblo era of the Pueblo III period (AD 1100s–1260s), when sites were situated near canyon heads to help control access.

This route description begins with Fish Canyon, but it is possible to hike it in either direction, starting with Fish or Owl Canyons. Hikers take note: beyond the first few miles in either direction the trail is neither well-marked nor defined due to natural processes, especially flash floods.

Experience with routefinding, scrambling, and bush-whacking are essential. The Fish-Owl Loop offers a striking world of red sandstone towers, glimmering pools of spring water, and remnants of the people who came here first. With this in mind, do your absolute best to select routes that do not "bust the cryptobiotic crust" (see **Respect Bears Ears**, page 14-15), use well-defined paths or trails when available, and do not alter the environment to make your way. This route is strenuous, at times technical, and only recommended for experienced and very fit hikers.

GETTING THERE: From Blanding, take US Highway 95 to County Road 261. Look for the Kane Gulch Ranger Station 4.0 miles down CR 261 for information, restrooms, and permits (which can also be paid for at the trail head). One mile past the ranger station take a left turn on the dirt road directing to the Fish Canyon/Owl Canyon Trailhead. Continue down this road for 5.0 miles until it ends at the trailhead. Campsites and restrooms are available here.

THE ROUTE: For the clockwise route, start at the Fish Canyon trailhead and take the left trail, which is clearly marked "Fish Canyon." For 1.5 miles, travel on a mostly flat, sandy, and well-defined single-track trail through a piñon and juniper forest. The trail leads to the Fish Canyon rim, which greets you with scenic vistas of the Bears Ears plateaus, Cedar Mesa, and of course Fish Canyon below. This is an ideal turnaround spot for hikers looking for an easy and short route.

To take on the full 17-mile loop, proceed to the canyon rim via the trail and look for a fixed rope to assist downclimbing into the canyon. Be sure to check that both the rope and rock

Owl Canyon will delight your senses with every twist and turn.

are in good condition. Do not pull on rocks that may crumble or fall off. To continue into the canyon, follow the cairns down the slickrock until you reach the floor, where you will pass by the first spring/pool.

Fish Canyon contains water from natural springs after winter snow melt (April through May) and during monsoon season (July through October), but be sure to bring plenty of water and filtering options as water levels and conditions can vary significantly day to day. This part of Fish Canyon follows a well-defined single-track trail and cairns. It crosses over several rock washes, so beware of slick mud and quicksand. Be sure to resupply with ample water before reaching lower Owl Canyon, which tends to have the least amount of water on the route and can become extremely hot with minimal shade.

The route eventually steers right after approximately 10 miles toward the confluence with Owl Canyon. This is where routefinding and knowledge of desert features is imperative. Cross over the creek and veer right toward Owl Canyon. There are faint trails in both directions, so it is possible to

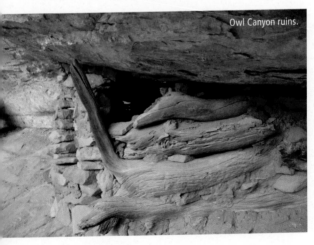
Owl Canyon ruins.

Nevills Arch.

get confused here if you are not paying attention. In 2017, the majority of Owl Canyon's trail was non-existent due to flash flooding. Select the most direct and efficient path that causes the least damage, but be warned—you will encounter cacti and thorny foliage.

Without a clear trail, natural geological landmarks are your best bet to find your way. You will encounter a series of three "falls" mid-way through Owl and some scrambling is necessary to get around and over these. At the third pool, head toward the canyon wall and find a set of cairns to guide you upward along the canyon walls, over and around the falls.

From here, rejoin the trail until you reach a diversion in the canyon that is not well-marked. Head to the right toward the exit of upper Owl Canyon where the route begins to climb and scramble over slickrock and boulders. When you reach the final rim of the canyon, be sure to stop and admire the prehistoric structures tucked just beneath the alcove. Ascend the canyon via a final scramble and follow the trail signs back to the parking lot/trailhead 0.25 mile away.

TRAILHEAD

Grand Gulch Overview

Grand Gulch, considered the "crown jewel" of Cedar Mesa, is a designated Wilderness Study Area (WSA), and is part of the original Bears Ears National Monument boundaries. Grand Gulch has numerous entrance and exit points with Kane Gulch, Toadie Canyon, Sheiks Canyon, and Bullet Canyon being the most common.

A loop hike is suggested to fully experience the canyon, using two different canyons as entrance and exit points. This requires a two car shuttle or road walking. Very fit trail runners should be able to cover such loops in a full day. Either a longer backpacking trip or multiple day-hikes is advised for anyone looking to explore each tributary of Grand Gulch.

While several springs and pools are sprinkled throughout the canyon, water levels vary drastically throughout the year (and even day to day), so hikers should be prepared to carry plenty of water and back-up filtration systems for travel through Grand Gulch. Pay close attention to weather conditions as the flash flood danger in this canyon is high and a quick exit is not possible (see **Flash Flooding**, page 16). If you are camping overnight, be sure to select an already established campsite situated on higher ground out of the direct path of flash flood terrain.

Grand Gulch is a premier hiking destination in Bears Ears.

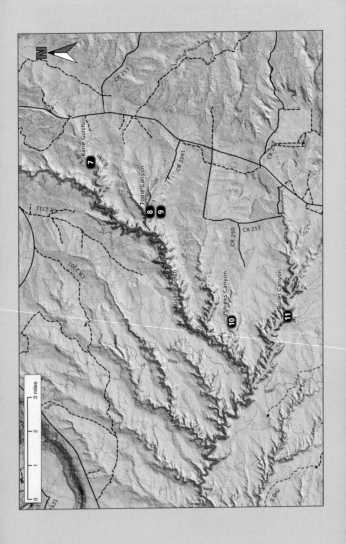

7. Kane Gulch

RATING:	Moderate
DISTANCE:	7.6 miles round-trip
ELEVATION CHANGE:	1,000 feet
ROUND-TRIP TIME:	Half-day or multi-day if extended into Grand Gulch
MAP:	Trails Illustrated Grand Gulch, Cedar Mesa Plateau
NEAREST LANDMARK:	Kane Gulch Ranger Station
NOTE:	Permit required; no dogs allowed

COMMENT: Kane Gulch is a gentle and intuitive starting point for most routes into the Grand Gulch Primitive Area. The confluence of Kane Gulch and Grand Gulch is incredibly scenic, with lush plant life flourishing between the curves of towering sandstone walls and overhangs, in addition to housing Junction Ruin. The trail itself is not very technical, with plenty of hard-packed single-track, slickrock, and washes,

Kane Gulch.

Spring in my step and in bloom around Junction Ruin during May—peak season for visiting Grand Gulch and its tributaries.

but there are several very rocky sections where hikers should watch their footing.

Depending on the time of year, especially late spring and just after summer monsoon season, water may be available from the stream. That said, one should travel well-prepared with plenty of water and back-up filtration systems. Pay close attention to weather conditions as the flash flood danger in this canyon is high and a quick exit is not possible. Budget your energy, water, and food to give yourself plenty of time to explore the details of each cultural site and rock art.

GETTING THERE: From Blanding, take US Highway 95 to County Road 261. Turn left on CR 261 and continue for 4 miles until you reach the Kane Gulch Ranger Station on the left. Walk across CR 261 from the permit kiosk to begin the route.

From Mexican Hat, drive north on US 163 for 3.9 miles and turn left (north) on UT 261. Follow UT 261 for 29 miles until you reach the Kane Gulch Ranger Station on your right.

THE ROUTE: After you cross CR 261, follow the flat single-track trail to a cattle gate. Be sure to close the gate behind you, regardless of how you find it. Continue along the trail for about 0.5 mile until the route becomes slickrock marked by cairns within Kane Gulch.

Weave your way through winding sandstone walls.

The trail begins to wind through a narrow overgrown section of brush, willows, and scrubs. During the first mile, Kane Gulch begins to look more like a canyon as you hike between white walls streaked black from rainfall. You will begin a rocky descent just before 2 miles to enter the Grand Gulch Wilderness Study Area. The downhill grade steepens until you reach a pour-off into the wash; stick to the slickrock cairned side here. Cross the wash and climb onto the north/northwest ledges. Enjoy stunning views below and beyond into Grand Gulch before a steep descent to the Kane Gulch canyon floor. Follow the cairns across the slickrock, over and around pools of water.

At about 3 miles, Kane Gulch veers west to reach the confluence with Grand Gulch at approximately 3.8 miles. Refill your water at Junction Spring and watch for the spur trail that leads to Junction Ruin a quarter mile farther.

Junction Ruin sits high on the right side of the trail in a north facing alcove. There are remains of many structures here including kivas, living rooms, and storage structures. Junction Ruin also holds pictographs and petroglyphs, and there are a number of hand prints on the canyon wall that were created by both positive and negative methods.

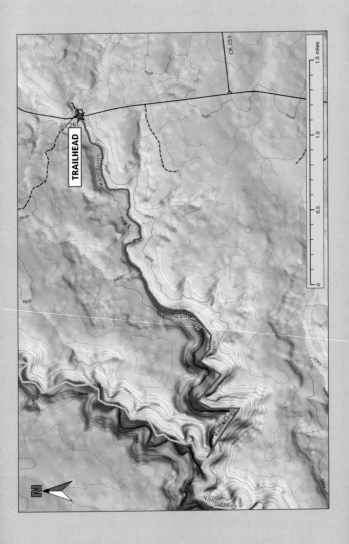

KANE GULCH

8. Toadie Canyon

RATING:	Difficult and strenuous
DISTANCE:	4 miles round-trip
ELEVATION CHANGE:	1,500 feet
ROUND-TRIP TIME:	Half-day or multi-day if extended into Grand Gulch
MAP:	Trails Illustrated Grand Gulch, Cedar Mesa Plateau
NEAREST LANDMARK:	Kane Gulch Ranger Station
NOTE:	Permit required; no dogs allowed

COMMENT: Toadie Canyon is a short but steep and technical entrance point for Grand Gulch. The steep sandstone walls (dropping 500 feet below the rim) and ruins tucked high above in its walls make it an interesting destination on its own.

This hike leads down Toadie Canyon to Grand Gulch, with Split Level Ruin as the destination. Keep your eyes out for several other sites along the way. For those looking for a longer or more comprehensive route, Toadie Canyon and Grand Gulch can be completed as a loop when connected with another canyon entrance such as Kane, Sheiks, or Bullet (see **Grand Gulch Overview**, page 71).

Toadie canyon is tough, technical, and worth the effort.

The entrance to Toadie Canyon requires Class 3 scrambling over boulders and slickrock switchbacks. The return back up this canyon, especially if wearing a heavy backpack, is strenuous and difficult. Do not attempt this route unless you are familiar, experienced, and comfortable with this type of terrain. Always check weather conditions and be alert for flash flood warnings (see **Flash Flooding**, page 16).

Although Toadie Canyon is short and follows a streambed at its bottom, water levels vary considerably and it can become quite dry for most of the year, so plan ahead and bring plenty of water and a filtration system.

GETTING THERE: From Blanding, take US Highway 95 to County Road 261 and go left. Stop at the Kane Gulch Ranger Station for information, permits, and restrooms. Continue south until you reach CR 2361 (this is just before mile marker 25) and go right, following this road for just over 1.0 mile.

From Mexican Hat, drive north on US 163 for 3.9 miles and turn left (north) on UT 261. Follow UT 261 until just past mile marker 25 and go left on CR 2361. Proceed with directions as above. The trailhead is 29.5 miles from Mexican Hat.

THE ROUTE: From the trailhead, follow the single-track trail that occasionally passes over sections of slickrock marked by cairns. At just over 0.5 mile, look for a series of cairns on the right marking the route to descend into the canyon. Follow the cairns that switchback over slickrock into the canyon floor.

From here, follow the single-track until you reach the confluence with Grand Gulch and continue to the left (south). Once in Grand Gulch, keep an eye out on your right for ruins, especially Split Level Ruin, which features an impressive two levels, an intact thatched roof, and a well-preserved kiva. If continuing to Sheiks Canyon, look for upwards of 11 archaeological sites on this stretch of Grand Gulch.

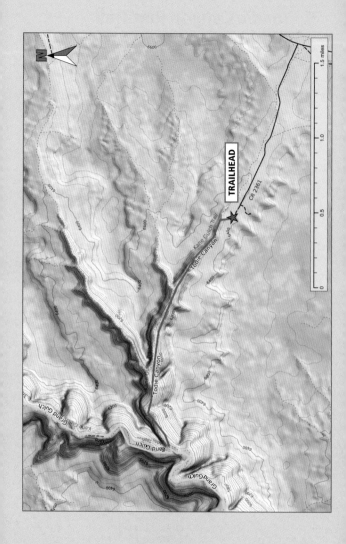

N

TRAILHEAD

CR 2381

Kane Gulch Trail

Toadie Canyon

Toadie Canyon

Grand Gulch

Kane Gulch/Grand Gulch - 3 mi.

Grand Gulch

6600

6400

6400

6400

6400

6400

6600

6600

0   0.5   1.0   1.5 miles

9. Toadie Canyon Rim Trail

RATING:	Easy
DISTANCE:	4 miles round-trip
ELEVATION CHANGE:	Less than 50 feet
ROUND-TRIP TIME:	Short day hike or run
MAP:	Trails Illustrated Grand Gulch, Cedar Mesa Plateau
NEAREST LANDMARK:	Kane Gulch Ranger Station

COMMENT: The Toadie Canyon Rim Trail is a delightful and flat route along well-maintained single-track and flat slickrock with sweeping views of Toadie Canyon, dropping nearly 500 feet below the rim. One mile into this hike, look

Looking rim to rim at the Bears Ears.

A route fit for the entire pack!

for a view of ruins on the other side of Toadie Canyon. Bring your own water on this route as there are no natural sources readily available.

GETTING THERE: From Blanding, take US Highway 95 to County Road 261 and go left. Stop at the Kane Gulch Ranger Station for information, permits, and restrooms. Continue south until you reach CR 2361 (just before mile marker 25) and go right, following this road for just over 1 mile.

From Mexican Hat, drive north on US 163 for 3.9 miles and turn left (north) on UT 261. Follow UT 261 until just past mile marker 25 and go left on CR 2361. Proceed with directions as above. The trailhead is 29.5 miles from Mexican Hat.

THE ROUTE: From the trailhead, follow the single-track trail that occasionally passes over sections of slickrock marked by cairns. As you pass through fragrant juniper and piñon forests, look across Toadie Canyon at 1 mile (this area is clear of brush and on slickrock) for an impressive view of ruins tucked high into the canyon walls with the Bears Ears mesas framing the background. Continue on for 1 more mile to a set of larger cairns that form an obvious lookout point with views into the Grand Gulch and Toadie Canyon confluence.

N

TRAILHEAD

CR 2361

Toadie Rim Trail

Toadie Rim Trail

Toadie Rim Trail

Kane Gulch

Grand Gulch

6400

6000

6200

6400

| 0 | 0.1 | 0.2 | 0.3 | 0.4 | 0.5 miles |

10. Sheiks Canyon

RATING:	Strenuous
DISTANCE:	6.0 miles rountd-trip
ELEVATION CHANGE:	2,000 feet
ROUND-TRIP TIME:	Half-day or multi-day if extended into Grand Gulch
MAP:	Trails Illustrated Grand Gulch, Cedar Mesa Plateau
NEAREST LANDMARK:	Kane Gulch Ranger Station
NOTE:	Permit required; no dogs allowed

COMMENT: Sheiks Canyon is home to the Yellow House Ruins, Green Mask Ruins/Pictograph Panel, and numerous other petroglyphs, pictographs, and carvings. At the Green Mask site, the highest-up images on the big rock art panel are from the Archaic period, thousands of years ago, and rock art from almost every subsequent culture phase is also represented,

The view of Sheiks Canyon after the confluence with Grand Gulch.

Yellow House Ruin.

ranging from at least 4,000 BC to AD 1200s. Both sites make this hike a worthwhile destination in itself but it is also an ideal entrance point to Grand Gulch. See **Grand Gulch Overview** (page 71) for more information about this area and route alternatives. Note that this route requires some Class 2–3 scrambling over boulders. It is not recommended for anyone inexperienced or uncomfortable with this terrain.

GETTING THERE: From Blanding, take US Highway 95 to County Road 261 and go left. Stop at the Kane Gulch Ranger Station for current information, permits, and restrooms. At mile marker 25, go left (west) on CR 250 for 3.1 miles. At this junction go right to stay on CR 250 until you reach the end of the road with the trailhead and parking area a total of 4.9 miles from CR 261.

From Mexican Hat, drive north on US 163 for 3.9 miles and turn left (north) on UT 261. Follow UT 261 and make a left

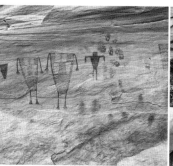

The rock art at the Green Mask site in Sheiks Canyon is some of the most detailed and well-preserved in all of Bears Ears National Monument.

turn on County Road 250 at mile marker 25. Proceed with directions as above.

THE ROUTE: From the parking area follow the remnants of the dirt road until it becomes a single-track trail. The trail soon fades out into the wash, which you will follow downstream. After 0.25 mile, look for the Yellow Roof Ruins tucked just under the canyon rim on the right (north). Continue down the wash using the cairns as guides through wide slickrock sections and occasional single-track that is overgrown with thick brush.

About midway, you will begin to encounter larger boulders and steeper expanses of slickrock marked by cairns. The route traverses a bench and then descends to the stream and takes you to the Green Mask Ruins and rock art site.

For those continuing on to Grand Gulch (either making a loop with another canyon or as a longer out and back), continue to follow the single-track trail as it winds around a curve in Sheiks Canyon to meet with Grand Gulch. At the confluence look for a rock formation known as "The Thumb" and just behind it the Cave and Wall Ruins tucked into an alcove along the north wall of Grand Gulch.

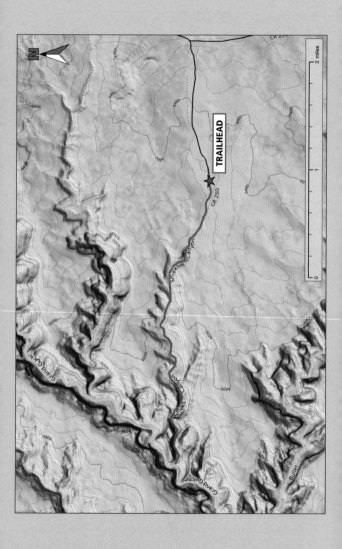

TRAILHEAD

11. Bullet Canyon

RATING:	Moderately difficult
DISTANCE:	13.4 miles round-trip
ELEVATION CHANGE:	2,000 feet
ROUND-TRIP TIME:	Full-day or multi-day if extended into Grand Gulch
MAP:	Trails Illustrated Grand Gulch, Cedar Mesa Plateau
NEAREST LANDMARK:	Kane Gulch Ranger Station
NOTE:	Permit required; no dogs allowed

COMMENT: Bullet Canyon is home to one of the Perfect Kivas (partially restored, the other one is in Slickhorn Canyon) and Jailhouse Ruin (named for the wooden latticed window high up on the rim of the canyon walls about mid-way through the route). Consult **Respect Bears Ears** (page 14-15) before exploring these sites.

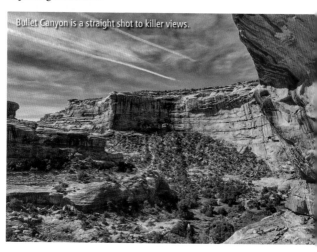

Bullet Canyon is a straight shot to killer views.

Note the T-shaped doorway on the structure just behind the kiva. T-shaped doorways first appeared in Chaco Canyon great houses and then dispersed throughout the region following the end of the Chaco era (AD 1150–1200s). No one is entirely sure of the reason for the T-shape. Kivas are thought to be ceremonial meeting places, according to ethnographic analogies with modern Pueblo groups. At Jailhouse Ruin, used for habitation and storage, the bright white "shield" insignia behind the narrow walkway on the upper level is thought to be more intimidating than ritual, intended to warn people not to get too close.

This is the largest tributary of the Upper Grand Gulch and can be made into longer loops when connected with Grand Gulch and its other tributaries (see **Grand Gulch Overview**, page 71). Bullet Canyon does require Class 3 scrambling at points, please use your best judgment and only take on this route if you are comfortable and experienced with this type of terrain. Several primitive campsites are available within the canyon as well as outside the trailhead.

The view into Bullet Canyon from the Perfect Kiva Ruin.

A reconstructed ladder at the Perfect Kiva.

Intricate rock art at the Jailhouse Ruin.

Always check weather conditions and be alert for flash flood warnings (see **Flash Flooding**, page 16).

Water levels within the canyon are variable (always carry your own supply) and the route can become quite hot due to lots of exposure and little to no tree growth or shade. Plan ahead and bring plenty of water and a filtration system.

GETTING THERE: From Blanding, take US Highway 95 to County Road 261. The Bullet Canyon sign will be on your right; turn right on CR 251 for 1.0 mile to the trailhead.

From Mexican Hat, head north on US 163 for 3.9 miles and turn left (north) on UT 261. Take UT 261 north for 21.7 miles and turn left (west) on the dirt road to Bullet Canyon, which is between mileposts 22 and 21 (there is a BLM sign marking the road to Bullet Canyon). Continue on the dirt road (County Road 251) for 1.2 miles to the trailhead.

THE ROUTE: The upper Bullet Canyon Trail begins above the canyon rim before descending a somewhat steep rocky section, marked with cairns, into the streambed at the mouth of Bullet Canyon. Follow the clearly marked trail, which hugs the stream for about 1 mile, until you reach an opening in

The desert is a symphony leading us back towards our own nature so that we can be a part of the music.

the gorge that descends along a dry fall. Follow the cairns and the curve of the canyon itself. The trail continues to be marked by cairns as it stays high on a bench on the north rim and then descends a rocky slope back to the canyon floor along the streambed.

Depending on the season, there may be streambeds and springs along the floor but DO NOT rely on this for water. As the canyon walls grow steeper (800 feet at their highest) the floor begins to widen and the trail runs through a flat, open, and grassy stretch. Keep your eyes open for clearly marked side trails that will lead you to the Perfect Kiva and Jailhouse Ruin between 4.5 and 5 miles. Keep in mind that these side trips will add 1–2 miles to your original route and some routefinding is necessary as well to locate the cultural sites (which is the fun part).

The lower canyon becomes brushier and more overgrown as it approaches Grand Gulch along a flowing stream. You will pass a dry fall above a deep pool during a shadeless stretch that also contains several more cultural sites. Turn around and head back to the trailhead or continue on for a longer multi-day route at the Grand Gulch junction or Sheiks Canyon.

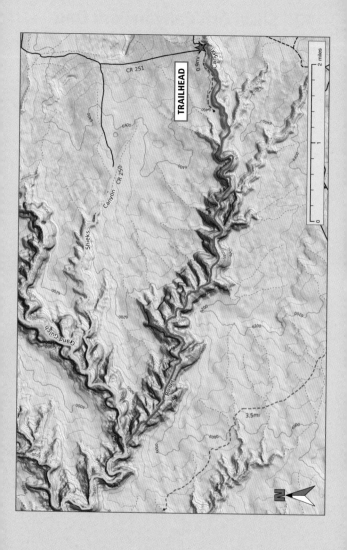

CR 251

TRAILHEAD

0.9mi

Canyon

6400

6400

6400

Shieks Canyon CR 250

6200

6200

6200

6200

Grand Gulch

6000

6000

6000

6000

Bullet

6400

6000

6000

6000

6000

6000

3.5mi

N

0 1 2 miles

12. Slickhorn Canyon Fork One

RATING:	Difficult
DISTANCE:	8.2 miles round-trip
ELEVATION CHANGE:	1,000 feet
ROUND-TRIP TIME:	Full-day hike
MAP:	Trails Illustrated Grand Gulch, Cedar Mesa Plateau
NEAREST LANDMARK:	Kane Gulch Ranger Station
NOTE:	Permit required, dogs not allowed

COMMENT: Slickhorn Canyon is known as the meanest and least explored canyon in Bears Ears. There are six forks leading into Slickhorn Canyon, with four main forks most commonly used for entry. Slickhorn Canyon is a tributary of the San Juan River, which eventually drains into Glen Canyon.

Balance the desire to look up at the views with watching your steps!

Slickhorn Canyon beckons those looking for an adventure across technical terrain.

While the first fork of Slickhorn is fairly short and is clearly marked both by cairns and, at times, defined single-track this is by no means an easy hike.

This guide presents routes for the first and fourth forks of Slickhorn because they are the most direct and well-travelled routes into this rugged area. It is up to you whether to explore these forks individually as out and backs, connect them with side trips to the other forks, or create a loop with another fork (a car shuttle may be necessary). Choose your own adventure!

Fork One contains a small granary in an alcove on the north side of the canyon at the beginning of the hike as well as the well-preserved Perfect Kiva, which still has an intact roof (a different Perfect Kiva exists in Bullet Canyon). When discovered, the structure held its original entrance ladder, but the BLM replaced this with a fabricated ladder. The original ladder can be viewed at the Edge of the Cedars Museum. Tree-ring data samples taken in 2016 date Perfect Kiva to 1246! As with all historical sites and artifacts on these routes, visit with respect and leave no trace.

A collection of potsherds—look but don't take! Hikers should never create these piles.

The Perfect Kiva in Slickhorn Canyon still has the original intact roof.

Slickhorn Canyon Fork One should not be attempted by anyone who is not well versed and quite comfortable with Class 2-3 terrain and routefinding. Bring plenty of water and filtration systems, but don't count on finding water to filter.

GETTING THERE: From Blanding, drive 9.4 miles south of the Kane Gulch Ranger Station on Highway 261, then turn right (west) on County Road 245/Slickhorn Road (between mileposts 19 and 20 and directly across from Cigarette Springs Road). Continue for 2.5 miles. At the major junction, stay left (south) for 1.6 miles and park on a faint side road just 0.1 miles farther.

From Mexican Hat, head north on US 163 for 3.9 miles and turn left (north) on UT 261. Continue on UT 261 for 19.1 miles and turn left (west) on County Road 245/Slickhorn Road. Follow the directions above.

THE ROUTE: From the trailhead, dip into the mostly slickrock wash until it joins a faint single-track trail that meanders in and out of it. Here you may wish to scramble up to the bench just above the wash to view a set of granaries beneath the alcove. Be sure to scramble back the same route from which you came, as this bench eventually cliffs out, making descent impassable even for strong climbers.

A hike through Bears Ears will walk you into the past.

At just over 1.5 miles the wash ends and dramatically drops into a pour-off. Look here for a set of cairns leading up and over the bench on the opposite side of the wash. At approximately 2 miles, the cairns begin to descend into the canyon. The rock at times is quite steep and loose. Be careful! Once on the canyon floor, keep your eyes open for a set of cairns that will guide you up the north side of the canyon to Perfect Kiva. If you choose to turn around here, the hike will be just under 5 miles.

To continue to the confluence with Slickhorn Canyon proper, follow the path in and out of the wash for another 3.5 miles down canyon where the trail leaves the wash and crosses over a grassy bench in the canyon floor.

Just before 4 miles, a "balanced rock" (page 92) will appear high up on the right (west/northwest) wall of the canyon. This typically makes a nice turnaround point for out-and-back hikes, unless your curiosity piques you to continue on to Fork Four or to explore the second and third forks, which are not described in this guidebook.

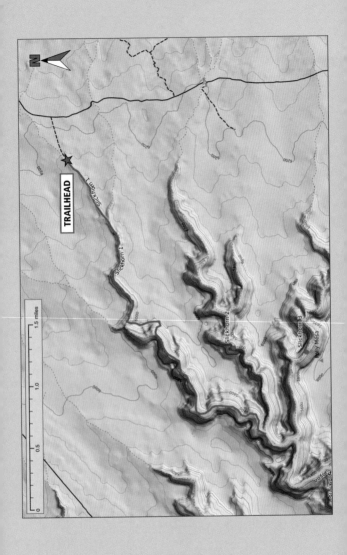

SLICKHORN CANYON FORK ONE

13. Slickhorn Canyon Fork Four

RATING:	Difficult
DISTANCE:	7 miles round-trip
ELEVATION CHANGE:	2,500 feet
ROUND-TRIP TIME:	Full-day hike
MAP:	Trails Illustrated Grand Gulch, Cedar Mesa Plateau
NEAREST LANDMARK:	Kane Gulch Ranger Station
NOTE:	Permit required; no dogs allowed

COMMENT: Slickhorn Canyon Fork Four is also known as the Sixth Fork or Trail Fork. This is a fun and challenging route that mixes slickrock, Class 3–4 scrambling, and rolling single-track, making it a nice challenging out-and-back day hike. Combine this route with the Fork One for a 10-mile,

Let the canyon walls engulf your sense of wonder.

one-way hike (this requires a car shuttle, bicycle, or plan to walk the approximately 4.5 miles between trailheads).

Slickhorn Canyon Fork Four should not be attempted by anyone without strong rock scrambling and routefinding skills. Bring plenty of water and filtration systems, but don't count on finding water to filter.

GETTING THERE: From Blanding, drive 9.4 miles south of the Kane Gulch Ranger Station on Highway 261, then turn right (west) on the County Road 245/Slickhorn Road (between mileposts 19 and 20 and directly across from Cigarette Springs Road). Continue for 2.5 miles. At the major junction, stay left (south) on County Road 203 for 5.7 miles. Turn right on an unmarked dirt road that passes a corral. After approximately 0.2 miles, at the end of the road, there is a parking area for the Trail Fork Slickhorn Canyon Trailhead.

From Mexican Hat, head north on US 163 for 3.9 miles and turn left (north) on UT 261. Continue on UT 261 for 19.1 miles and turn left (west) on County Road 245/Slickhorn Road. Follow the directions above.

Slickrock is a classic element of desert terrain in Bears Ears.

▲ Granary structures like this were used for food storage by the ancient Puebloans.

◀ Sandstone walls are good for the heart and soul.

THE ROUTE: From the corral, follow the old tire tracks until they become a single-track trail that drops into the canyon while it is still shallow, at just under 1 mile (note the granary ruin tucked under the canyon rim). Follow the cairns down canyon as they meander in and out of the wash.

It is most important on this route to pay attention to the cairns and the topography as the route cliffs out at several pourovers and large boulder fields. If you find yourself at a cliff, get your bearings, look for cairns or an alternative route, and when necessary, back track until you return to the designated path.

As you near the confluence, expect to navigate through thick sections of overgrown brush. From the confluence at approximately 3.5 miles from the trailhead, take advantage of the spring that is rumored to hold water year round. Then either turn around and retrace your route or continue on to return through Slickhorn Canyon Fork One.

TRAILHEAD

Slickhorn 4

Slickhorn 4

Slickhorn 3

Polly Mesa

Slickhorn Canyon

N

0   0.5   1.0   1.5 miles

Dark Canyon Overview

Dark Canyon's beauty is often compared to the Grand Canyon. A trip to Bears Ears is not complete without a hike along this corridor. The shortest, and most technical, approach into Dark Canyon is via the Sundance Trail (approximately 4 miles each way), however most hikers opt to make Dark Canyon a multi-day trip by combining two different canyons into a loop as entrance and exit points. A more comprehensive one-way Dark Canyon trek requires a two car shuttle.

Water levels vary widely in each tributary and lower Dark Canyon, while upper Dark Canyon tends to be dry. Hikers should come prepared with at least one gallon of water per person per day, a water filtration/treatment system, and skills in seeking out natural desert water sources such as springs, hanging gardens, and small pools (see **Dehydration/Heatstroke**, page 18). When camping overnight, be sure to select an already established campsite situated on higher ground out of the direct path of flash flood terrain.

Don't let the name deceive you—the light dances passionately within the deepest recesses of Dark Canyon.

14. Woodenshoe Canyon

RATING:	Moderately difficult
DISTANCE:	29.6 miles round-trip
ELEVATION CHANGE:	7,000 feet
ROUND-TRIP TIME:	2–3 days
MAP:	Trails Illustrated Manti-La Sal National Forest
NEAREST LANDMARK:	Bears Ears

COMMENT: Woodenshoe Canyon is a tributary of Dark Canyon that cuts through South Elk Ridge. Expect to find lush foliage, towering red sandstone canyon walls, cliff dwellings dating between AD 1100–1200s, and arches here in one of the most remote corners of Bears Ears.

For those looking for a longer route (most likely for an overnight backpacking trip), Woodenshoe Canyon is 14.8 miles

Allow the expansive scenery of Bears Ears to let you feel small.

long, making it a 29.6-mile out-and-back route. It can be made into a longer loop when combined with Dark Canyon and another tributary like Peavine Canyon. Or make a one-way traverse of Dark Canyon using a car shuttle exit via the Sundance Trail. An 8.0 mile one-way hike (16 miles out and back) into Woodenshoe Canyon will take you to the heart of the canyon for one long day hike or a manageable overnight backpacking trip.

GETTING THERE: From Blanding, drive south on UT 191 (Main St.) for just under 4 miles and turn right on UT 95. Continue for 30 miles until you reach UT 275/Natural Bridges National Monument and go right (north). Continue for 0.7 miles and take the first available right, 088 Elk Ridge Road, and drive 7.9 miles. Take a sharp left onto County Road 256/County Road 268/Forest Road 108 (Dry Mesa) for 2.0 miles. Then go left on Deer Flat Road for 1.7 miles. Finally, make a right onto Woodenshoe Point Road 340 for 0.9 miles until you reach the Woodenshoe Trailhead.

The dramatic contrasts of red sandstone cliffs, ancient dwellings, and high elevation forests.

Woodenshoe Canyon offers a long hike far from the "real" world.

THE ROUTE: The elevation drops very quickly on this route with the steepest sections in the first 3 miles. The narrow trail is shaded with ponderosa pine, Douglas fir, aspen, and Gambel oak.

Just before 5 miles the trail veers east and reaches a crossroads between Woodenshoe Canyon and Cherry Canyon (heading east). Take the trail toward Woodenshoe Canyon and cross the streambed. Within the next 1.0 mile experience the contrast of the 1,200-foot sandstone canyon walls against the blue sky and the lush flatlands through which you are hiking.

The next 1 mile reveals Keyhole Arch Canyon on the east (to see the Keyhole Arch travel off the Woodenshoe route into Keyhole Arch Canyon for 1.5 miles). For those continuing on to Dark Canyon, look for a wooden trailhead sign at the confluence directing various routes to Peavine and lower Dark Canyon (Lake Powell).

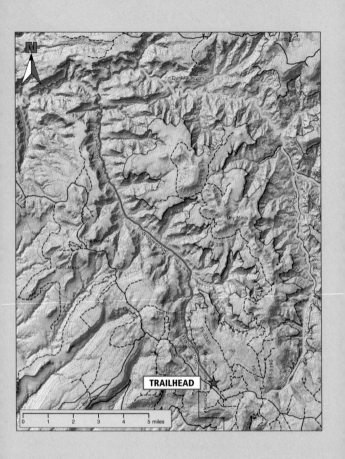

TRAILHEAD

15. Peavine Canyon

RATING:	Moderate
DISTANCE:	26 miles round-trip (Peavine Canyon is 13 miles one way for hikes linking up with Dark Canyon.)
ELEVATION CHANGE:	4,500 feet
ROUND-TRIP TIME:	2–3 day
MAP:	Trails Illustrated Grand Gulch, Cedar Mesa Plateau
NEAREST LANDMARK:	Bears Ears

COMMENT: Peavine Canyon is classically combined with Dark Canyon and Woodenshoe Canyon to form the "Dark Canyon Loop," which is approximately 40 miles long. The Peavine Canyon and Woodenshoe Canyon Trailheads are less than 3 miles apart making even a solo trip with one car feasible and car shuttles a snap. Peavine Canyon is an advantageous

Peavine Canyon is a gentle, forested approach to reach Dark Canyon.

The mountainous landscape of Elk Ridge is exemplified in Peavine Canyon.

entrance or exit point to stock up on water for the habitually dry upper Dark Canyon.

GETTING THERE: From Blanding, drive south on UT 191 (Main St.) for just under 4 miles and turn right on UT 95. Continue for 30 miles until you reach UT 275/Natural Bridges National Monument and go right (north). Continue for 0.7 miles and take the first available right, Elk Ridge Road (Forest Road 088) and drive 7.9 miles, climbing the pass to the Bears Ears mesas. Here the road becomes CR 88/228. Turn left at the junction onto FR 108/San Juan County Road 256, signed Woodenshoe–6. Follow FR 108 west, parking at the signed Peavine Trailhead after 1.9 miles.

THE ROUTE: From the trailhead, follow the single-track path that generally follows the creek descending into the canyon. Be aware of wildlife and cattle seeking water in this area, as upper Dark Canyon tends to be dry. If you are continuing on past Peavine into Dark Canyon (and even if you plan to connect with Woodenshoe, which also has some water), be sure to stock up on fluids before you reach the confluence (always filter and treat your water) as there is a rather long and dry stretch between the two canyons.

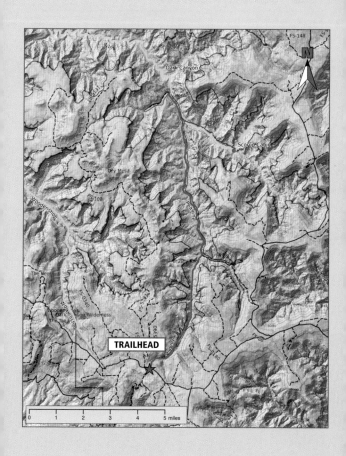

TRAILHEAD

0   1   2   3   4   5 miles

16. Sundance Trail

RATING:	Strenuous
DISTANCE:	8 miles round-trip (The Sundance Trail is 4.0 miles one way for hikes linking up with Dark Canyon.)
ELEVATION CHANGE:	3,000 feet
ROUND-TRIP TIME:	Half-day hike
MAP:	Trails Illustrated Manti-La Sal National Forest
NEAREST LANDMARK:	Lake Powell

COMMENT: The Sundance Trail is the shortest and one of the most travelled entrance points into lower Dark Canyon—but don't let that fool you, it is also strenuous and technical. The complete route should only be taken on by the fittest of hikers experienced with loose and rocky Class 2-3 terrain. The first 2 miles along the rim of Dark Canyon are extremely scenic, with panoramic views of Dark Canyon and its confluence

Stop and appreciate the views into Dark Canyon on your way down the Sundance Trail.

below, which also can be a day hike. The Sundance Trail also serves as an excellent entrance or exit point for various longer and multi-day routes in Dark Canyon (see **Dark Canyon Overview**, page 101). There is no water on the Sundance Trail until you reach the floor of Dark Canyon, and the route is fully exposed—come to this hike prepared with plenty of fluids and aware of the hazards of heat exhaustion.

GETTING THERE: From Blanding, take a right on UT 95 and continue for approximately 70 miles. Take a right off the highway onto the dirt road between mile markers 48 and 49. After 4 miles, the road joins with Horse Tanks Road (Forest Road 2081 (208A); continue for another 3.5 miles and stay left on Squaw Rock Road. In approximately 4 more miles you will see signs for the Sundance Trailhead. Go left at the junction and continue for 1 mile where the road ends at the junction.

THE ROUTE: From the trailhead/parking area the Sundance Trail begins with a gentle 300 feet of elevation gain and loss, pristine footing via Jeep road, groomed single-track, and

In Bears Ears, the word "trail" is a loose term at best. Always pack along your route finding skills.

cairned slickrock (with a bit of Class 2–3 scrambling to keep things interesting).

Past this point the trail descends a steep (12% grade), loose talus slope, dropping 1,120 feet into the canyon in less than 1 mile. While cairns mark the route, there is no clear path and routefinding, scrambling, and experience on this type of terrain is imperative. You may find entrance into the canyon to be more difficult (keep your balance) than the return ascent (which is strenuous), especially if you are carrying a heavy pack. Once at the bottom of the slope, follow the cairn-marked boulder field across the canyon where it rejoins the single-track trail that leads to the creek at the bottom of Dark Canyon and to the lower Dark Canyon Trail junction, if you are continuing for a longer hike.

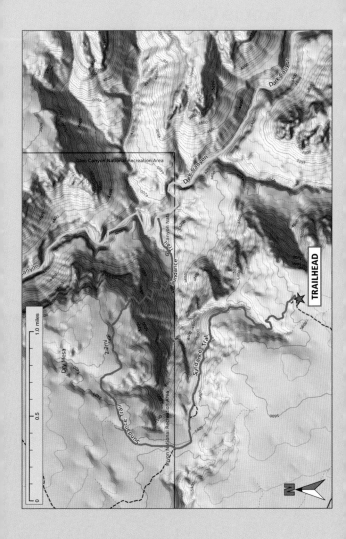

17. Scorup Cabin

RATING:	Moderate
DISTANCE:	8.2 miles round-trip
ELEVATION CHANGE:	3,000 feet
ROUND-TRIP TIME:	Half-day hike
MAP:	Trails Illustrated Manti-La Sal National Forest
NEAREST LANDMARK:	Bears Ears

COMMENT: This day hike begins atop the forested Elk Ridge (8,599 feet elevation) and descends to the floor of Horse Pasture Canyon, where it ultimately connects with Dark Canyon. Near the end of Horse Pasture Canyon is Scorup Cabin, the recommended turnaround point for this day hike, which was used historically as a cabin both for oil drilling

The natural beauty surrounding Scorup Cabin is the true masterpiece.

Scorup Cabin.

workers and cowboys. Scorup Cabin was originally located in Rig Canyon (on the other side of Dark Canyon), and was associated with the historic oil rig for which that canyon was named. After the oil rig was decommissioned, the cabin was taken apart and rebuilt at its current location by Al Scorup, around 1930, so he could use it in his big cattle outfit.

GETTING THERE: From Blanding, drive south on UT 191 for just under 4 miles and turn right on UT 95. Continue for 30 miles until you reach UT 275/Natural Bridges National Monument and go right (north). Take the first right on Elk Ridge Road (Forest Road 88), paying close attention to the hairpin turn in the road at the junction with FR 92. From this point, continue 11.4 miles to the Horse Pasture Trailhead (FR 25) on the left. Go left at the fork and continue until you reach the official trailhead.

THE ROUTE: From the trailhead, follow the clear-cut single-track trail across the wooded bench above the canyon. The route begins to descend at just over 0.5 mile. As the descent steepens, the trail switchbacks down the canyon with sweeping views of high sandstone walls and rock formations. When

The window seat view of Horse Pasture Canyon from inside Scroup Cabin.

you have reached the canyon floor at just under 3 miles, continue along the valley floor and follow the extremely faint boot-beaten path through lush green reeds. While the route is not specifically or clearly marked, it is easy to follow if you stay between both main canyon walls. When you reach a cattle fence at just over 3 miles, begin to look for views of Scroup Cabin on your left, at 4.1 miles.

The descent into Horse Pasture Canyon.

18. Hammond Canyon

RATING:	Moderate
DISTANCE:	13 miles round-trip
ELEVATION CHANGE:	4,500 feet
ROUND-TRIP TIME:	Full-day hike
MAP:	Trails Illustrated Manti-La Sal National Forest
NEAREST LANDMARK:	Bears Ears

COMMENT: With its garden of desert towers and massive sandstone walls tucked among the forests that flank Elk Ridge, a hike down Hammond Canyon exemplifies the beauty hidden within every nook of Bears Ears, which can unfortunately be missed by those who never pull off the highway and start

Hammond Canyon is a magical kingdom of sandstone castles and desert towers.

For trail runners, Hammond Canyon offers one of the most runnable routes within Bears Ears National Monument.

walking! This route is 6.5 miles each way on a well-defined and easy to follow trail, making it an excellent route for anyone looking for a traditional hike or trail run (just good old-fashioned walking on dirt) in Bears Ears. While the creek at the bottom of Hammond Canyon provides ample water at times throughout the year, always come prepared with your own supply and filtration/water treatment system.

GETTING THERE: From Blanding, drive south on UT 191 for just under 4 miles and turn right on UT 95. Continue for 30 miles until you reach UT 275/Natural Bridges National Monument and go right (north). Take the first right on Elk Ridge Road (Forest Road 88) paying close attention to the hairpin turn in the road at the junction with FR 92. Continue on FR 88 until you reach the sign for the Hammond Canyon Trailhead on your right. Make the turn and continue down the short road to the trailhead.

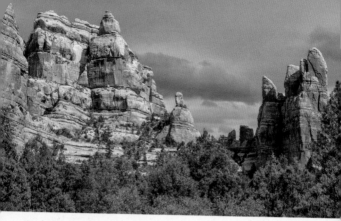

Sandstone castles await your visit.

THE ROUTE: From the Hammond Canyon Trailhead, follow the single-track trail across a flat, grassy, forested area until it begins its steep descent into the canyon. The trail remains rocky and steep for about 2 miles until reaching the canyon floor where it flattens out along the creek bottom and is quite clear. It is one of the easier routes in Bears Ears to follow. Continue along the trail until you reach the sign marking the confluence of Hammond Canyon and Posey Canyon. It is possible to link Hammond Canyon and Posey Canyon if you have a car shuttle, but note that Posey Canyon can be more difficult to follow.

Let your imagination run wild.

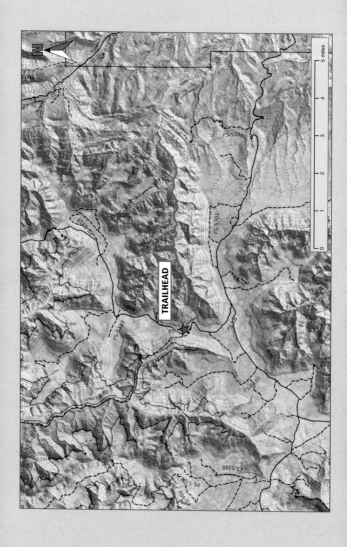

TRAILHEAD

19. Wolfman Panel and Ruin

RATING:	Moderately easy
DISTANCE:	1.0 mile round-trip to panel; 1.4 miles round-trip to a nearby ruin
ELEVATION CHANGE:	350 feet
ROUND-TRIP TIME:	Short day hike
MAP:	Trails Illustrated Grand Gulch, Cedar Mesa Plateau
NEAREST LANDMARK:	The town of Bluff

COMMENT: The Wolfman Panel is a highly detailed set of petroglyphs featuring distinct images of a man, a shield, a mask, a bird, a plant, and other objects. Enjoy using your imaginations to decipher these remarkable symbols—their meaning remains a mystery. Another archaeological conundrum is the twinlobed circles featured on the rock art panel. They occur

These ancient images are clear but their meaning is a mystery.

Leaping over the edge of past and present.

frequently throughout the Bears Ears area, and nobody is quite sure what they represent. Unfortunately this beautiful site has recently been vandalized with bullet holes and graffiti—a sobering reminder to respect these historical sites, to take nothing with you, and to leave no trace on your visit.

Across the wash there is a small ruin, also with a petroglyph panel. While the exact dates for this site are unknown, archaeologists estimate this structure once used for storage dates back to probably AD 1100s or 1200s, and much earlier for the rock art.

GETTING THERE: From Bluff, take US 191 south for 4.2 miles and continue straight on Highway 162 for 0.9 miles. Turn right on CR 262, Lower Butler Wash Road, between mileposts 40 and 41. Take the road north for 1.0 mile until you reach a spur on the left just before a cattle guard.

From Mexican Hat, head east on US 163 for 19.6 miles and turn left on CR 262, Lower Butler Wash Road. Take the road north for 1.0 mile until you reach a spur on the left just before a cattle guard.

Lifestyles of the ancient
Puebloans home tour.

Butler Wash.

THE ROUTE: From the BLM sign on Butler Wash Road, walk west down the dirt Jeep road. Continue past the "No Vehicles" sign. The dirt will become slickrock—keep going. Head toward yet another "No Vehicles" sign (this one also has a wooden blockade). Keep your eyes open for cairns and follow them toward the east rim of the wash. If you look directly across the wash, you will see a set of ruins tucked beneath the west rim.

Veer left/south along the rim (you are 0.25 mile from the start at this point) looking for another set of cairns perched atop a rock, which mark the route to descend into the wash. It will be the most obvious route as much of the rim is completely cliffed-out and not passable for hikers. Pass between the narrow space between the boulder and a larger slickrock wall.

Next, find a mild stair-step scramble over a few boulders leading to an obvious slickrock ramp. Stay along the canyon edge nearest the rock walls and head toward an alcove, which you will cross beneath. Just around the bend find the Wolfman Panel petroglyphs against the sandstone wall. To view the nearby small ruin, follow the faint trail across the wash and through the dense brush, which may be difficult to navigate, if not impassable at times, due to unmaintained growth.

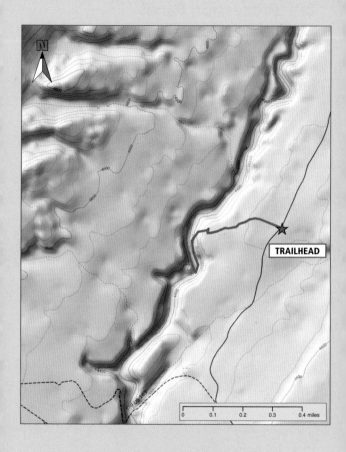

TRAILHEAD

0   0.1   0.2   0.3   0.4 miles

20. Procession Panel

RATING:	Moderately easy
DISTANCE:	3.0 miles round-trip
ELEVATION GAIN:	510 feet
ROUND-TRIP TIME:	Short day hike
MAP:	Trails Illustrated Grand Gulch, Cedar Mesa Plateau
NEAREST LANDMARK:	The town of Bluff

COMMENT: The Procession Panel is a stunning 15-foot-long expanse of rock art that is tentatively dated to the Basketmaker III period, although this is currently up for debate as the Panel continues to be studied.

The view of Comb Ridge across from Butler Wash will put its 80-mile length into perspective.

Cattle crossing.

Cairns mark this moderately easy short hike, but hikers be warned: a slip from the cliff edges on portions of this hike would prove fatal. The final ascent to Procession Panel also requires moderate scrambling over medium sized boulders. In addition, this route is highly exposed with no shade and water—arrive prepared with fluids and plan to complete this route during cooler times of the day to avoid heatstroke. As with all artifacts and historical sites within this guide, plan extra time to enjoy the Procession Panel and adhere to the **Respect Bears Ears** tips (page 14-15).

GETTING THERE: From Bluff, take US 191 south for 4.2 miles and continue straight on Highway 162. Continue on Hwy 162 for just under 1 mile. Turn right on CR 262, Lower Butler Wash Road, and reset your odometer (this is important because the trailhead is unmarked). The trailhead will be on your left 6.6 miles from the highway.

Continue exploring past Procession Panel to enjoy views like this.

From Mexican Hat, head east on US 163 for 19.6 miles and turn left on CR 262, Lower Butler Wash Road, and follow the rest of the directions above.

THE ROUTE: From the trailhead, follow the clear single-track trail that cuts through some trees and a shallow wash for 0.5 mile before climbing up onto the exposed slickrock that comprises the majority of this hike. The route is marked by cairns heading directly upward on the west/southwest side of the canyon ridge toward a break in the ridge before descending to the canyon floor, where the route rejoins a single-track path (you will reach a trail signpost in this section).

Keep your eyes open for cairns 1.2 miles into the hike to guide you up along the south ridge to the Panel. This section requires some moderate scrambling over boulders. The Procession Panel will be on your right with sweeping views of Comb Ridge, southern Bears Ears National Monument, and even Monument Valley.

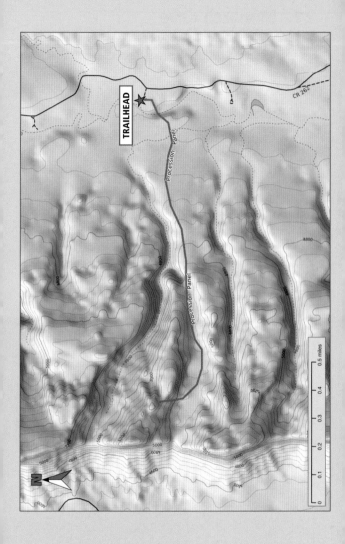

TRAILHEAD

Procession Panel

Procession Panel

CR 261

N

0   0.1   0.2   0.3   0.4   0.5 miles

21. Monarch Cave

RATING:	Moderately easy
DISTANCE:	2 miles round-trip
ELEVATION CHANGE:	400 feet
ROUND-TRIP TIME:	Short day hike
MAP:	Trails Illustrated Grand Gulch, Cedar Mesa Plateau
NEAREST LANDMARK:	The town of Bluff

COMMENT: Monarch Cave is tucked within Comb Ridge, and the name dates back to a historic inscription from the 1892 Illustrated American Exploring Expedition. Beneath the beautiful large alcove remain ancestral dwellings, pictographs, and petroglyphs from the Pueblo III era (AD 1150–1260s). Enjoy exploring the well- preserved ruins, rock

Monarch Cave still retains its regal features.

Ancient artwork adorns Monarch Cave.

The land still speaks for its indigenous inhabitants.

art, and a colorful dripping spring at the back of the cave. Please visit this and all cultural/historical sites in Bears Ears with the utmost respect. Given its short distance and proximity to both the Wolfman Panel and Procession Panel, these hikes can be completed in succession over one to three days.

GETTING THERE: From Bluff, take US 191 south for 4.2 miles and continue straight on Highway 162. Continue on Hwy 162 for just under 1 mile. Turn right on CR 262, Lower Butler Wash Road, and reset your odometer (this is important because the trailhead is unmarked). The trailhead will be on your left about 7.2 miles from the highway.

From Mexican Hat, head east on US 163 for 19.6 miles and turn left on CR 262, Lower Butler Wash Road. Proceed to the route following the same directions as above.

THE ROUTE: From the trailhead, the route begins with a single-track path into the wash, across and up its steep sandy slope. The trail follows the sandy rim of the wash before descending into the canyon. Once in the canyon, follow the well-worn path along the floor. When the cave comes into view just above the canyon floor, follow the cairns that lead up to the ruins.

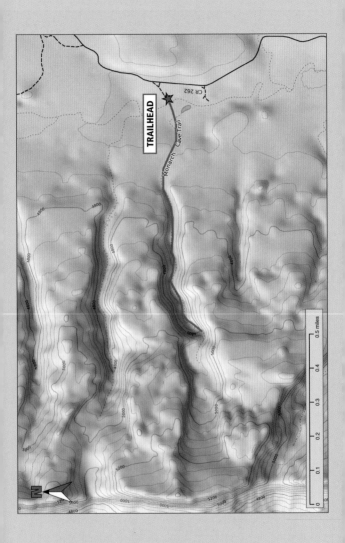

TRAILHEAD

Monarch Cave Trail

CR 262

0.5 miles

0   0.1   0.2   0.3   0.4   0.5 miles

N

22. Lower Indian Creek Trail and Newspaper Rock

RATING:	Moderately easy
DISTANCE:	13.2 miles round-trip
ELEVATION CHANGE:	2,000 feet
ROUND-TRIP TIME:	Half-day hike
MAP:	Trails Illustrated Manti-La Sal National Forest
NEAREST LANDMARK:	Newspaper Rock or Monticello

COMMENT: This is your chance to hike directly from the Abajo mountains to the desert terrain of Indian Creek and experience the drastic contrasts of Bears Ears National Monument. Either the start or the middle of your route (depending on your starting point) will take you to the Newspaper Rock Petroglyph Panel.

The wingate sandstone walls that line Indian Creek make this area a world renowned rock climbing destination.

Newspaper Rock

Newspaper Rock is unique in that it presents a wide variety of rock art styles from both the Ancestral Puebloan and Fremont civilizations, as this portion of Bears Ears served as "the border" between the two cultures. Experts suspect that the Fremont "Barrier Canyon" and the Basketmaker "San Juan Anthromorphic" pictograph styles share a common root in this area. During periods of peaceful trade, it is likely that items such as beans, ceramics, and the bow-and-arrow passed from the Basketmaker III people to the forebears of the Fremont.

This route has substantial water (always bring along a filtration device), good shade, and gentle terrain. Indian Creek and the Abajo Mountains are rich with wildlife, including bears!

GETTING THERE: From Monticello, go west on 200 South and stay left when it splits into a Y at Abajo Dr./Hart's Draw Road. Continue on Hart's Draw Road for 12.0 miles and turn left on Forest Road 100 (Indian Creek). At 1.1 miles you will reach Foy Lake/Spring Lake; turn right on Forest Road 104 (Shay Ridge) and continue for 3.0 miles to Lower Indian Creek Trail #21.

TO START AT NEWSPAPER ROCK: Drive south from Moab on Highway 191 for 40 miles until you reach HWY 211. Take a right here and continue for 12.0 miles. There will be a sign alerting you that Newspaper Rock is approaching in 500 feet. Park in the designated area for Newspaper Rock, but take note that you will need to walk along the highway for just under 0.5 mile, crossing two cattle guards; keep an eye out for a cattle gate on the right (south) side of the road.

THE ROUTE: Almost this entire route meanders along the Indian Creek on a clearly worn single-track path. As you begin your descent in the Abajo Mountains at 7,434-feet, notice the red rock walls that begin to emerge from the canyon as it drops to 6,430 feet. The trail widens considerably at around 5.5 miles and you will reach a BLM gate at approximately 6.2 miles.

Go left at the gate on the dirt shoulder of the highway. You will cross two cattle guards before you reach the Newspaper Rock National Monument parking area. Cross the road here and proceed to the petroglyph panel. Be sure to pace yourself to reserve energy for the return trip, which climbs gradually uphill to the higher elevation in the Abajo Mountains. (If you are beginning this hike at Newspaper Rock, simply reverse these directions and note that you will climb uphill for the first portion of the route and descend back to your vehicle).

This well-maintained trail is a perfect entry-level hike and is also accessible for mountain bikes, motorcycles, and equestrian travel.

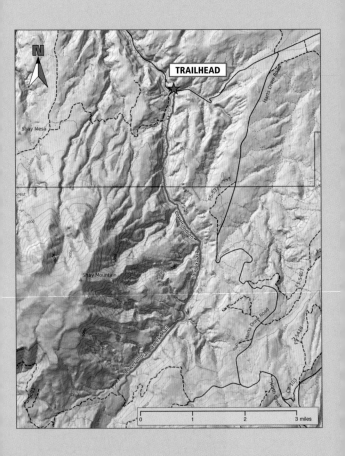

23. Skyline Trail / Tuerto Canyon Loop

RATING:	Moderately strenuous
DISTANCE:	10.9 miles total
ELEVATION CHANGE:	6,000 feet
ROUND-TRIP TIME:	Half-day hike
MAP:	Trails Illustrated Manti-La Sal National Forest
NEAREST LANDMARK:	The town of Monticello

COMMENT: Nestled in the high-elevation Abajo Mountains, which rise to 11,000 feet, the Tuerto Canyon Loop is a stunning route. It weaves on mountain trails in and out of oak and aspen groves, sandstone canyons, and mountain ridgelines with incredible views extending to the Bears Ears, Elk Ridge,

The Abajos are also known locally as the "Blue Mountains".

Palette of autumn colors.

Cattle grazing is permitted in Bears Ears National Monument for ranchers with preexisting contracts.

Comb Ridge, Indian Creek, and even Canyonlands National Park. While the loop is not technical, be advised that the trail can be faint and hard to follow at times, many trail signs have fallen or been destroyed (so be sure to bring a map and this guidebook), and the additional elevation can have a substantial effect on even the fittest hikers coming from sea level. Be sure to give yourself at least one night at a higher elevation to adapt, drink plenty of water, and pace yourself to account for the additional exertion you may experience.

This route can be accessed from roughly late spring to early winter, making it a great summer hike as the mountains offer cooler temperatures and relief from flash flooding in monsoon season. But note that Tuerto Canyon itself is in the flood zone and lightning is a concern, so consult the **Flash Flooding** (page 16) section before this and all other routes. Perhaps the most striking time to hike in the Abajos is during fall, when leaf colors on the aspens, oaks, and Gambel oaks peak in a vibrant seasonal display.

This loop begins at the Skyline Trailhead off Forest Road 95, just before The Causeway, and ends at the Tuerto Canyon Trailhead approximately 0.3 mile from the start, making it easy to return to your car via the road. It is also possible to connect this route with the Shay Ridge/Tuerto Canyon Loop

The peaks of the Abajos rise up to 11,368 feet.

(8.5 miles) as a figure eight. As with all routes in this book, the loop described here is merely a suggestion, and many variations are possible among the extensive trail network in the Abajos.

GETTING THERE: From Blanding, head east on Center Street and take the first left (north) onto 100 E (CR-285) and travel 1.7 miles. Continue to Blue Mountain Rd. (Causeway 095) and travel about 19 miles. You will see a sign on your right for the Skyline Trailhead. One-quarter mile farther is the Tuerto Canyon Trailhead.

THE ROUTE: Beginning at the Skyline Trailhead off FR 95 follow the single-track route that quickly ascends along the ridge. This trail climbs substantially, and at around 2 miles becomes faint and more difficult to follow, so pay attention. The trail works its way slightly left and under a small summit. At 2.5 miles find the conspicuous junction with Trail #13 (Allen Canyon Blue Creek Trail). Take this trail slightly left of the Skyline Trail to complete the loop described here.

Fall colors paint the Abajos at magic hour.

Leaf no trace.

Continue up the ridgeline about 0.5 mile following the very large cairns on the Blue Creek/Allen Canyon Trail until the trail splits. Take a left into the trees and pass through a national forest gate.

From here, the trail descends another 2 miles through obvious single-track before converging with the Blue Creek/Tuerto Trail #14. Go left and hike the wide ridgeline between canyons for about 1.5 miles before the trail ends at its junction with the Tuerto Canyon Trail #11. Head south at this junction, which takes you to the canyon floor where there may be water access.

The trail then climbs out of Tuerto Canyon and over and past Trough Canyon and its trail junction. Stay on the Tuerto Canyon Trail #11 until you arrive at the Tuerto Canyon Trailhead on FR 95, about 0.33 mile from where you started. Follow FR 95 back to your car.

TRAILHEAD

24. Shay Ridge Trailhead/ Tuerto Canyon Loop

RATING:	Moderately strenuous
DISTANCE:	8.5 miles total
ELEVATION CHANGE:	4,000 feet
ROUND-TRIP TIME:	Half-day hike
MAPS:	Trails Illustrated Manti-La Sal National Forest
NEAREST LANDMARK:	The town of Monticello

COMMENT: The Shay Ridge Trailhead/Tuerto Canyon loop can be viewed as a sequel or companion to the Skyline/ Tuerto Canyon Loop—with such incredible views of Bears Ears paired with the mountainous terrain, it is enticing to stay for one more route. This is also a great option for those looking to approach from the northern side of the Abajos via

Be patient at altitude—pace yourself, stay hydrated, and pause to take in the views.

The high point of Bears Ears contrasts with the red rock desert of Indian Creek and Canyonlands below.

Monticello, rather than from the south via Blanding. To cover longer distances, it is also possible to connect this route with the Skyline Trail/Tuerto Canyon. Many other variations or loops exist among the many miles of trails in the area.

GETTING THERE: From Monticello, go right (west) onto 200 South and stay left when it splits into a Y at Abajo Drive/Hart's Draw Road. Continue on Hart's Draw for 12 miles and turn left on Forest Road #100 (Spring Lake) for over one mile. Turn right onto FR #104 (Shay Ridge) for 6 miles until you reach Shay Ridge Trail #162 on your left.

THE ROUTE: Start at the Shay Ridge Trailhead along the Jeep road. You will soon go through a fence with signs for Tuerto Canyon Trail #11, which will quickly descend a steep and rocky slope losing nearly 1,000 feet of elevation in one mile (pace yourself—you will climb back up this same route on your return). At the bottom follow the cairned and singletrack route crossing the seasonal creek. After a short climb you will arrive at the Blue Creek Allen Canyon Trail #13 junction.

Aspen groves are unique in that each individual tree is part of one collective organism.

Bears (Ears) poop.

The route described here goes left here and returns via the trail to your right. From the junction the trail will climb steadily, eventually passing a large cattle pond. Arrival at a series of cabins indicates that you are about to join with the Blue Creek/Tuerto Canyon Trail #14.

Just past the cabins, the trail cuts across a large meadow, then descends the wide ridgeline between two canyons for about 1.5 miles. This trail ends at its junction with the Tuerto Canyon Trail #11. Take a right and head north descending back into the canyons. The route will roll up and down (but mostly down) until you arrive at the junction where you started the loop. Return to the trailhead climbing the same steep rocky trail that you came in on.

TRAILHEAD

Blue Creek Point

| 0 | 0.5 | 1.0 | 1.5 miles |

25. Fable Valley

RATING:	Moderate
DISTANCE:	24 miles round-trip
ELEVATION CHANGE:	3,000 feet
ROUND-TRIP TIME:	Overnight
MAP:	Trails Illustrated Manti-La Sal National Forest
NEAREST LANDMARK:	Bears Ears

COMMENT: Tucked into one of the most remote regions of Bears Ears National Monument, Fable Valley connects the Dark Canyon Plateau with Beef Basin. The route has many notable attractions, including numerous archaeological sites containing ruins and rock art. Read **Respect Bears Ears** (page 14-15) carefully before your visit to ensure that these areas remain in a condition for others to enjoy and for researchers to study.

A journey to the remote Fable Valley rewards your effort.

The confluence of Fable Valley and Gypsum Canyon.

While a large portion of this route takes you along the valley floor, several miles traverse the canyon rim, offering sweeping and dramatic views of Fable Valley below and its confluence with Gypsum Canyon. The hike covers a substantial distance but the trail is very smooth, relatively easy to follow, and mostly flat (except for the 3 miles each way to enter and exit the valley), making this a feasible full-day hike for strong trekkers and a lovely overnight trip for most. Although water can be found in Fable Valley post-monsoon season, it can be unpredictable (and paired with hot temperatures especially in summer), so bring plenty of water and materials to filter and treat water.

GETTING THERE: From Blanding, drive south on UT 191 for just under 4.0 miles and turn right on UT 95. Continue for 30.0 miles until you reach UT 275/Natural Bridges National Monument and go right (north). After 0.75 mile take the first right on Elk Ridge Road (Forest Road 88). Pay close attention to the hairpin turn in the road at the junction with Forest Service Road 92, taking a sharp left here to stay on Elk Ridge Road. From this point continue on FR 88 until you reach FR 91, North Long Point Road. Turn left here, which is 5.0 miles

The walls of Bears Ears have stories to tell.

A room with a view of Fable Valley.

north of the now burned-down Gooseberry Guard Station. Continue down FR 91 (North Long Point Road) for approximately 0.25 mile until you reach the sign for the Fable Valley Trailhead on your right, and park here.

THE ROUTE: This route begins at the Fable Valley Trailhead sign. Due to the rough nature of the road past the sign, it is not advisable to take your vehicle beyond this point. The hike on the road to the official Fable Valley Trailhead is 2 miles each way. From the wooden gate at the end of the rough four-wheel-drive road continue to the single-track, which begins to steeply descend into the valley.

Once on the canyon floor the trail continues across the brushy confluence and cuts across to the northeast side of the valley. The trail follows the valley floor until its confluence with a large canyon on your right, where it picks up again on the northeast side and dramatically improves.

Protect and enjoy what you love.

At around 8.5 miles the trail cliffs out at a very large water-fall, which is dry most of the year, and has a hanging garden below. If you reach this point, you will need to backtrack just a bit to regain the trail, which gradually climbs the eastern walls of the canyon to begin its traverse of the rim. This point makes a natural spot for day-hikers to turn around, while overnight backpackers will continue. The dramatic canyon views from atop the rim are not to be missed and are worth the effort to hike up there.

For those continuing, follow the cairns along the rim trail. The trail follows the eastern and southern rims of both Fable and Gypsum Canyons, and offers breathtaking views of both canyons and their confluence. The trail then once again meanders in and out of sandy washes and is marked by cairns ending at the other end of the Fable Valley Trailhead, about 3.5 miles from the large waterfall. While it is certainly possible to drive to this northern trailhead to begin your hike, it is considerably farther removed from other routes in Bears Ears and the roads are not maintained and generally only accessible by ATV.

About The Author

Morgan Sjogren is a freelance writer and photographer whose storytelling focuses on human-powered exploration and wild landscapes. Sjogren's book debut, *The Best Bears Ears National Monument Hikes* (2018), was the first guidebook devoted to the original monument boundaries. In 2019, Morgan wrote *The Best Grand Staircase-Escalante National Monument Hikes* and *Outlandish: Fuel Your Epic.*

Illustration by Jesse Crock

Join Today.
Adventure Tomorrow.

The Colorado Mountain Club helps you maximize living in an outdoor playground and connects you with other adventure-loving mountaineers. We summit 14ers, climb rock faces, work to protect the mountain experience, and educate generations of Coloradans.

www.cmc.org